THE LYRIC
IMPULSE

❧

The Charles Eliot Norton Lectures

1964–1965

THE LYRIC

IMPULSE

C. Day Lewis

❧

Harvard University Press

CAMBRIDGE, MASSACHUSETTS

1965

Library of Congress Catalog Card Number
65–16682

Printed in the
United States of America

I wish to thank those authors and publishers who
have kindly permitted me to use copyrighted material, for which full acknowledgment has been made
in the Notes. My thanks are due also to publishers
and proprietors for permission to quote from the
following works: "The Shropshire Lad", (Authorized
Edition) from *The Collected Poems* of A. E. Housman (The Society of Authors, London; copyright
1940 by Holt, Rinehart and Winston, Inc.); *Complete Poems of Robert Frost* (copyright 1923, 1930,
1934, 1939, by Holt, Rinehart and Winston, Inc.
Copyright 1951, © 1958, 1962 by Robert Frost);
Collected Poems by Marianne Moore (The Macmillan Co., New York; copyright 1935 by Marianne
Moore, renewed 1963 by Marianne Moore and T. S.
Eliot; *Collected Poems* by W. B. Yeats (copyright
1919, 1933, 1934, by The Macmillan Co.; copyright
1940 by Georgie Yeats, renewed 1946, 1962, by
Bertha Georgie Yeats); *The Collected Poems* of
Thomas Hardy (Trustees of the Hardy Estate; copy-
right 1925 by The Macmillan Co., New York);
Colm O'Lochlainn, *Irish Street Ballads* (London:
Constable, 1939; New York: Corinth Books, 1960).

FOREWORD

The amount which most practitioners of poetry can say about their art is strictly limited. They will draw a few sweeping—often too sweeping—lines, then leave the scholar and the critic to fill in the picture. I am no exception to this rule. Throughout the lectures printed here, I was approaching my subject with the prepossessions and the limitations of a practising poet.

I would like first to thank Harvard University and the Charles Eliot Norton Committee for the great honour they did me in asking me to give these lectures. I thank the Master of Lowell House and Mrs. Stewart, and the tutors and undergraduates there, who gave such a heartwarming welcome to the stranger within their gates: my experience of living amongst them will remain, during the days that are left to me, one of my happiest memories. I received the same kindness from so many other Harvard faculty members that to enumerate them all would be to turn a foreword into a catalogue.

With a few small verbal alterations, the lectures are printed as they were delivered.

C. DAY LEWIS

❦

CONTENTS

THE LYRIC IMPULSE

1. THE LYRIC IMPULSE

The poet's reading is a desultory affair: with books as with other experiences—Robert Frost said it—poets "stick to nothing deliberately, but let what will stick to them like burrs where they walk in the fields."

A poet must believe that the momentousness, the significance, *to him*, of a book, a scene, a thought, a face, an event, will come to him, if ever it comes, by not examining it until he has slept on it—the maturing sleep in which raw experience suffers a sea-change, and from which it arises purged of impurities, refreshed, more malleable. His response to other men's poetry, too, will be a hand-to-mouth affair, in which his chief motive is not to formulate or assess, but a personal need, a need for mediation. He will get little from another man's work till he is ripe for it—ready, that is, to find in it something he needs, a use of language or a view of life which can fruitfully modify his style and direct him towards a better understanding of his own experience.

At any given time, the mediator can be a major poet, but equally he could be a minor one: think how many great things have grown from a seed planted in a writer by some work or passage of much smaller scope or merit. For this reason, as a practising poet at any rate, I have to be a relativist. I am not concerned with placing poets or poems in an order of merit, nor do I see much point in arguing whether it is valuable or even possible to do so. I am concerned with what a poem can give me, whether this be technical advice or spiritual encouragement, for my own work. The questions I ask a poem, or a genre of verse, will therefore be different from the questions asked by the critic. The genre I am dealing with is lyric poetry; and the reader will find in these pages, I dare say, a good many more questions than answers. But what I would most like him to do is to read and respond to a kind of poetry which today is under a cloud.

If we asked a man in the street, "What are lyrics?" he would probably reply that they are the words of songs sung by pop singers or the high spots in the book of a musical comedy. The mantle of the bard has fallen upon the shoulders of the pop singer—from which it is frequently torn off by a raving horde of his fans and distributed among them as souvenirs. Nothing new in this. The first pop singer, Orpheus, was torn in pieces by Maenads. And dare we feel superior about these rabid manifestations? Do they not indicate a psychological need, a spontaneity of emotion, which the higher levels of art in the West are today ignoring? William Empson has recorded a conversation with a young poet who "hated all the other ones his age. He was talking about one of these and I said, 'He has a singing line, hasn't he?' Meaning, as I thought, that he had the root of the matter in him. This chap pounced and said 'That's it, you've got it! Just a writer of lyrics!' "

One could not have a more naked exposure of the state of mind prevalent today amongst intellectuals. We shall have to ask ourselves whether 'the singing line' is now, to all the intents and purposes of serious poetry, ended; whether it can be renewed, and whether it ought to be. We have been taught to admire complexity, intellectual toughness, irony, sometimes to the exclusion of other poetic virtues. Is this right? Because we get so much from Donne, does it

mean we can get little or nothing now from Herrick? Has
the lyrical simplicity of a Herrick become a manner not
possible for contemporary poets?

I want to trace this 'singing line' through English poetry.
But first, some definitions. And these are curiously difficult
to make. Yet we must try to make them, unless we throw in
our hands and say that a lyric is any poem which is not
dramatic or epic or narrative or satirical, or that a lyric is any
poem of not more than about thirty lines. Yvor Winters,
who seems to call any short poem a lyric, tells us the lyric
is superior to all other forms of poetry because of "the
expository concentration of a motivating concept in language such that the motivating concept and motivated
feeling are expressed simultaneously and in a brief space."
I think we had better start again.

Let us start by distinguishing between the lyric and lyrical
poetry. A lyric is a poem written for music—for an existing
tune, or in collaboration with a composer, or in an idiom
demanded by contemporary song-writers, or simply with
music at the back of the poet's mind. Lyrical poetry is a
much looser thing, but it has not quite forgotten its origin in
music and has not lost the singing line: the liberation of the
lyric from music enabled the former to break away from
certain conventions, to expand, to treat a greater variety of
subjects, to explore deeper into poetic meaning—to be, in
fact, a lyrical poem. This is not the fidgety distinction it
may at first seem.

We think of the lyric as the purest and simplest form of
poetry. It is a poem which expresses a single state of mind, a
single mood, or sets two simple moods one against the other.
It does not argue or preach. If it moralises, the moral has
an unsophisticated, proverbial ring—'More geese than swans
now live, more fools than wise.' It speaks with no irony or
complexity of syntax: it is transparent, undiluted by any

cerebral matter, unclouded by afterthoughts or the reflection of individual personality. If we are unwary, we may also claim the lyric impulse as one which issues into verse of an absolute spontaneity, as a pure *cri de coeur:* We may even think of the lyric poet as a kind of bird. This is unwise: however much we may be lulled by phrases like 'a nest of singing birds' or 'native woodnotes wild', we shall soon have to snap out of it, for the poets themselves will indignantly tell us that there is no such thing as an artless poem.

A Canadian poet, appropriately named Robert Finch, wrote

> *And poetry is a song, when the bird has flown,*
> *About a bird, never the bird's own.*[1]

We know that while a reed bunting's song is innate, a linnet's is acquired from other linnets, and will never be acquired if the young bird is kept in isolation. Young chaffinches, at the period when their testes are maturing, will imitate the song of linnets or canaries if kept with them. Some birds do not have to learn their song; others do. We also know, incidentally, that when a cock-nightingale sings at night, it is not in ecstasy or pain, but because he needs to feed every three or four hours and his song is a warning, between meals, to other nightingales to keep off his feeding-ground.

Where man is concerned, there is an *element* of instinctive spontaneity in his song—an element Santayana pointed to when he wrote, 'The imagination is, as it were, the self-consciousness of instinct.' In writing a love poem, for instance, the poet is partly impelled by sexual instinct; but he is conscious of the states of mind this instinct produces in him, aware of himself feeling, and it is this primary self-consciousness which gives its imaginative depth and shape to the poem. We shall have to ask ourselves later whether the elaborate self-consciousness of modern man has not, by reaching an imbalance with his instinctual spontaneity, killed the lyric medium.

We must not, of course, confuse self-consciousness with sophistication. 'O Westron Wind' is a supremely unsophisticated poem, Rochester's 'All my past life is mine no more' a highly sophisticated one: but each is effective as a lyric because each is a poem which does not try to say more than one thing at a time, the former giving us a pure image of love-longing, the latter a light-hearted defence of inconstancy: the longing for one woman and the longing for many women are both common enough states of mind. This saying of only one thing at a time, without reservations, modifying parentheses, mental complications of any kind, is the lyric's chief term of reference.

Brevity, simplicity, purity. What about impersonality? We may think of the lyric, today, as the most personal, intimate kind of poem. But if we look back at the great age of English lyric-writing—the period roughly between 1560 and 1620, we shall have to revise our opinion. Although the style of Campion, say, is fairly easily distinguishable from the style of John Fletcher, the difference remains a matter of style: we are not aware of a particular man writing out of his own individual personality and experience, as we are with a lyrical poem by Wordsworth or Hardy. This lack of personal flavour was due largely, not to any theories that the lyric should be impersonal, but to the discipline imposed on it by music. With the bulk of Elizabethan and Jacobean lyrics, what we hear is not this unique human being but Everyman singing through him. The attitude towards love, for instance, is a generalised attitude: any given love poem is likely to be a variation on one of the few accepted themes—Cupid's mischief, jealousy, self-pity, woman's disdain, her fickleness, her killing eyes; woman as a person intolerable to live with but even worse to live without: and she herself is not an individual woman so much as a generalised figure. It is not insincerity—sincerity does not come into it—but the convention which dictated that a poet should transmute his genuine ecstasy or agony into a stylised genre.

There are a few exceptions. Early in the century, Wyatt had written one poem which was a sport. Quite a number of his poems have the personal flavour we seldom find in Elizabethan lyric: but 'They flee from me that sometime did me seek' is something different—an intensely *private* poem, and a dramatic lyric: there is an immediateness of personal experience about it, a vividness, an indiscretion, which contrast strongly with the formalized manner of his successors.

> *They flee from me that sometime did me seek,*
> *With naked foot stalking in my chamber.*
> *I have seen them gentle, tame and meek,*
> *That now are wild and do not remember*
> *That sometime they put themselves in danger*
> *To take bread at my hand; and now they range*
> *Busily seeking with a continual change.*
>
> *Thanked be fortune, it hath been otherwise*
> *Twenty times better; but once, in special,*
> *In thin array, after a pleasant guise,*
> *When her loose gown from her shoulders did fall,*
> *And she me caught in her arms long and small,*
> *Therewith all sweetly did me kiss,*
> *And softly said 'Dear heart, how like you this?'*
>
> *It was no dream; I lay broad waking:*
> *But all is turned thorough my gentleness*
> *Into a strange fashion of forsaking;*
> *And I have leave to go of her goodness;*
> *And she also to use new-fangleness.*
> *But since that I so kindly am served,*
> *I fain would know what she hath deserved.*

Take just one word there—'With naked foot *stalking* in my chamber.' A contemporary poet, aiming at physical precision, might have said 'padding'—and created a tactless irony, raising up in our minds the image of some predatory Thurber-esque female. 'Stalking' is the gait of long-legged birds, and so prepares us for 'to take bread at my hand': it is also the gait of ghosts—Wyatt remembers these bodies 'in thin array' as phantoms of delight. But 'stalking' too implies stealthiness, the movement of the hunter; and one of these women at least, as the second stanza tells, was a shameless, active pursuer. All three connotations of 'stalking' were available to Wyatt, and I think he was aware of them: we certainly are.

The break-through Wyatt made here was not followed up—dramatic verse and psychological naturalism being kept for the theatre—until we come to Drayton's 'Since there's no help, come let us kiss and part', some of Shakespeare's sonnets, and John Donne's love poems. In 'They flee from me' Wyatt showed how much more weight and variety of tone the lyric poem could bear if it broke out of its conventional moulds. Donne was the first English poet (Catullus had done it in his time) to present in lyrical verse the whole gamut of sexual love—its tenderness and lust and exhilaration, the idealism *and* the disrespect.

To return now to the 'singing line'. There are in fact two lines, which sometimes interweave and at other periods have little or no contact: we could call them the lyric of the folk and the lyric of the few. Out of the folk emerge the ballads, which were story lyrics, the folk songs, and the carols. Whether these were composed by a bard attached to a nobleman's household, by a wandering minstrel, by some gifted village versifier, by a monk or a clerk, they are all anonymous, and they are all popular poetry in the sense that every member of a community could participate in them with enjoyment. By the end of the fifteenth century, the minstrels had virtually disappeared, their function of disseminating verse taken over by the invention of printing. Folk lyric, through chapbook and broadsheet, flourished for another three hundred years, then slowly faded into the Victorian street ballad, renewed itself in the music-hall and finally has become the pop song of our own time.

The lyric of the few began as a courtly amusement. It ramified in the great 1560–1620 period of the lutanists and the madrigal, when music was an accomplishment expected of every gentleman. At the beginning of the seventeenth century, however, the lyric divided, and more and more of its impulse was to flow into lyrical poetry. As yet, however, there was no irreparable cleavage into what we should now call popular art on the one hand and highbrow art on the other. There are many instances of Elizabethan and early Stuart composers' evolving their music from folksong themes: in Shakespeare's plays—*Othello, Lear* and *Hamlet,* for example—there are many snatches from popular ballads, or allusions to them. Later, the songs in Dryden's plays, the rollicking ditties of Gay, Sheridan, and Dibdin carry on the line of the lyric proper, while Byron's 'We'll go no more a-roving' was based on a well-known folk-song.

This cross-fertilisation between the folk lyric and poetry for the few has not entirely ceased even now: Mr. T. S. Eliot's references to popular song in *The Waste Land,* his study of music-hall as a help towards the re-creation of popular drama, are an instance of this. The need for lyric poetry to renew contact with its origins in the folk is one which keeps cropping up. The Augustan age, for example, when little other serious poetry was written in lyric form, was the great age of hymn-writing—hymns that were both serious and widely accepted. The *Lyrical Ballads* of Wordsworth and Coleridge, again, were attempts to use a popular medium for exalted ends.

It was the misfortune of the Romantic poets that they lived at a time when there were no English composers of a talent to match their own; or perhaps we should call it the misfortune of the lyric. That close-working collaboration between poet and composer was ended, without which the lyric proper is a poem trying to hoist itself up by its own bootlaces. The song lyric lost impetus and conviction, gradually declining into the 'art-song' and the drawing-room ballad, seeping away into a morass of cliché and sentimentality, from which it was not rescued until, in the late Twenties and the Thirties of this century, there arose in America several writers who, working closely with composers, produced popular lyrics of genuine vivacity and distinction, in a truly modern idiom.

Keats and Tennyson had to wait for a century or more before a composer of genius, Benjamin Britten, set a few of their lyrics to music. A. E. Housman, whose lyrics cried out for tunes—and frequently got them—was quite indifferent to the musical setting of his work. Yeats, who had an incomparable ear for verbal rhythm, had none for the rhythms and tones of music. It may be that for some poets 'Heard melodies are sweet, but those unheard are sweeter': there is a sense in which one can fairly say that no one can write a good lyric without some melody, heard or dimly apprehended, in his head. Blake used to make up tunes for his lyrics and sing them to himself. There is this attraction towards music whether or no a poet resists it, whether or no he feels that his lyric is complete without it, because music is at the source of his tradition.

And, conversely, there has been the need to liberate himself from music so that the poem may say more, or say it differently. One can feel the language of lyric poets, even in the Elizabethan period, straining now and then at the leash. Reaching out towards the particular and unconventional in Campion's

> *Sooner may you count the stars*
> *And number hail down-pouring,*
> *Tell the osiers of the Thames*
> *Or Goodwin sands devouring,*
> *Than the thick-showered kisses here . . .*

Reaching towards the toughness and paradox of the Metaphysicals in Campion's

> *Turn all thy thoughts to eyes,*
> *Turn all thy hairs to ears,*
> *Change all thy friends to spies*
> *And all thy joys to fears . . .*

or in Dowland's 'I saw my Lady weep'—

> *Sorrow was there made fair,*
> *And Passion wise; Tears a delightful thing;*
> *Silence beyond all speech, a wisdom rare . . .*

Reaching towards a Metaphysical pertness of wit in John Fletcher's

> *Danaë, in a brazen tower,*
> *Where no love was, loved a shower.*

Straining, within the conventions of the song-lyric, towards a Donne-like frankness and naturalism, a disabused attitude to woman which should reverse, so to say, the decisions of the Courts of Love and expose the artificiality of their procedure:—

> *Thou art not fair, for all thy red and white,*
> *For all those rosy ornaments in thee;*
> *Thou art not sweet, though made of mere delight,*
> *Nor fair, nor sweet—unless thou pity me.*
> *I will not soothe thy fancies, thou shalt prove*
> *That beauty is no beauty without love.*

Yet love not me, nor seek not to allure
  My thoughts with beauty, were it more divine:
Thy smiles and kisses I cannot endure,
  I'll not be wrapped up in those arms of thine:
Now show it, if thou be a woman right,—
Embrace and kiss and love me in despite.[2]

Again, leaving aside Shakespeare's sonnets, which were
not written for music, we find in the lyric of the period, and
particularly in songs from plays or masques, another foreshadowing of the greater breadth of meaning which was to
come when the lyrical impulse freed itself from the direct
influence of music. Just here and there a line rises up and
speaks to us with a resonance far beyond what we expect
from the song lyric (it could be argued that the elegance of
a song is more likely to be impaired than enhanced by a
'great' line—it can be disproportionate, upset the balance).
I myself hear this particular resonance in such lines as these:
—the last line of this stanza from Surrey's 'Complaint of the
Absence of her Lover being upon the Sea'—

> *When other lovers in arms across*
>   *Rejoice their chief delight,*
> *Drowned in tears, to mourn my loss*
>   *I stand the bitter night*
> *In my window, where I may see*
> *Before the winds how the clouds flee:*
> *Lo! what a mariner love hath made me!*

> *Brightness falls from the air;*
>   *Queens have died young and fair.*
>
>   [Nashe]

> *Those are pearls that were his eyes:*
> *Nothing of him that doth fade*
> *But doth suffer a sea-change*
> *Into something rich and strange*
>
>   [Shakespeare]

A hyacinth I wished me in her hand.
[Drummond of Hawthornden]

Except Love's fires the virtue have
To fright the frost out of the grave.
[Jonson]

John Fletcher's apostrophe to 'Care-charming Sleep'—

Into this prince gently, oh, gently slide,
And kiss him into slumbers like a bride.

Vain the ambition of Kings
Who seek by trophies and dead things
To leave a living name behind
And weave but nets to catch the wind.
[Webster]

In each of these familiar passages the key line has a depth or strangeness or audacity of metaphor we might expect to find in the turbulent body of Elizabethan and Jacobean drama rather than in the songs which adorned it. The lyric of the period is for the most part a small, unambitious, polished thing: but now and then one of these gems took on an unwonted fire and force from its dramatic setting. There were various reasons why a playwright put lyrics into a play—W. H. Auden has written well about this in his *Homage to Igor Stravinsky*. The Elizabethan audience liked such entertainment; a dramatist wished the songs not merely to entertain but to have some dramatic relevance; the character who asks for a song will have some reason for wanting it; he needs distraction from a certain state of mind, or to indulge himself in it, or to seduce a woman, and so on.

But although such lyrics were created for a dramatic situation, it is possible to detach the best of them from their context without depriving them of lustre. We do not need to know the relevance of 'Take, oh take those lips away' in

Measure for Measure, to feel it as a tremendously powerful image of desertion. The poem is in this respect as self-sufficient as Burns'

> *Oh wert thou in the cauld blast*
> *On yonder lea, on yonder lea,*
> *My plaidie 'gainst the angry airt*
> *I'd shelter thee, I'd shelter thee.*

—lines which give us a pure image of every young man's protective tenderness for his beloved.

Association with great drama, then, helped to enlarge the scope of the lyric; and the decline of drama left a hole, so to speak, which was not entirely filled by the rising novel. The dramatic lyrics and monologues of Browning, Meredith's *Modern Love*, suggest what effective plays they might have written if they had had a living tradition of poetic drama to work in. As it was, from the late eighteenth century the lyric impulse became diffused over an ever-widening area, till today one could almost say there is no lyric poetry since every poem has a lyrical quality. The expansion of lyric into lyrical showed itself, not in a different balance between the personal and the impersonal, but as a general movement from objective to subjective. Collins' *Ode to Evening*, no more than Thomson's *The Seasons*, tells us primarily about the poet's state of mind, Wordsworth's nature lyrics, Keats' Odes are primarily about states of mind.

Paul Tillich can say, 'A modern work of art functions precisely to make the mind aware of itself; the reference is directly back to the individual.' A hundred and thirty years ago Tocqueville could say,

Thus not only does democracy make every man forget his ancestors, but it hides his descendants and separates his contemporaries from him; it throws him back forever upon himself alone and threatens in the end to confine him entirely within the solitude of his own heart.

The poet may rejoice in this solitude, or find in it a symbol
of the heroic—

> *The outward shows of sky and earth,*
> *Of hill and valley, he has viewed;*
> *And impulses of deeper birth*
> *Have come to him in solitude.*
>
> [Wordsworth]

> *A lonely impulse of delight*
> *Drove to this tumult in the clouds.*[3]
>
> [Yeats]

Or he may meditate upon it with regret and melancholy, as
did John Clare—

> *I am: yet what I am none cares or knows,*
>   *My friends forsake me like a memory lost;*
> *I am the self-consumer of my woes,*
>   *They rise and vanish in oblivious host,*
> *Like shades in love and death's oblivion lost;*
> *And yet I am, and live with shadows tost*
>
> *Into the nothingness of scorn and noise,*
>   *Into the living sea of walking dreams,*
> *Where there is neither sense of life nor joys,*
>   *But the vast shipwreck of my life's esteems;*
> *And e'en the dearest—that I loved the best—*
> *Are strange—nay, rather stranger than the rest.*
>
> *I long for scenes where man has never trod,*
>   *A place where woman never smiled or wept;*
> *There to abide with my Creator, God,*
>   *And sleep as I in childhood sweetly slept:*
> *Untroubling and untroubled where I lie,*
> *The grass below—above, the vaulted sky.*

Of that poem the distinguished neurologist, Lord Brain,
has said that as a description of the depressive state 'it might
well find a place in a textbook of psychiatry'. It is a *cri-de-*

coeur, but the kind in which the poet allows us to hear him brooding over his mental agony rather than gives us an image of it: a subjective poem, and also a highly personal one. Compare with it two poems on the same general theme of isolation, loss of innocence, madness—Blake's 'O Rose, thou art sick' and Crabbe's extraordinary ballad, 'Sir Eustace Grey': they too are subjective, but, unlike Clare's poem, distanced and impersonal. Crabbe and Blake were almost exact contemporaries: Clare was already in his thirties when they died. It is an indication of lyrical poetry's rapidly broadening scope that within this period three poems so utterly diverse in treatment could be written on closely related themes.

There is this horizontal enlarging—the power to treat a much greater variety of subjects in a greater variety of ways —which followed the divorce of lyric from music. There is also what I might call a vertical development—that is, the possibility of putting greater imaginative or emotional pressure behind lyrical poetry than the song-lyric was able to sustain. We have seen, in the lines of exceptional resonance which I chose from sixteenth and early seventeenth-century verse, a foreshadowing of this development: from the last quarter of the eighteenth onwards, it was running free. We are aware of a frightening violence behind Crabbe's 'Sir Eustace Grey'. We feel a different but no less strong imaginative pressure beneath most of Blake's *Songs of Experience:* it is as if certain poets had been able to break through to deeper levels in themselves, and harness the burning energy they found there into lyrical poetry. Richard Ellman has said of Yeats that all his middle and later poems sound as if they had been written for an emergency. Perhaps we go too far today in demanding that a poet should always be working at his top pressure—in dismissing such of his verse as is 'merely' graceful, accomplished, written from a relatively superficial level: but that is by the way.

This vertical development—the reaching to a greater height or depth of meaning—is exemplified in one of Wordsworth's 'Lucy' poems:—

> A *slumber did my spirit seal;*
>   *I had no human fears:*
> *She seemed a thing that could not feel*
>   *The touch of earthly years.*
>
> *No motion has she now, no force;*
>   *She neither hears nor sees;*
> *Rolled round in earth's diurnal course,*
>   *With rocks, and stones, and trees.*

The resonance of that little poem is achieved by a high pressure of emotion, by a simplicity of language which tautens this emotion, and by a simple contrast of related viewpoints. In the first stanza, Wordsworth is saying that, when Lucy was alive, he could not associate her with mortality. In the second, the position is reversed: it is Lucy now who is sealed in slumber: she, who "seemed a thing that could not feel/The touch of earthly years", is now at their mercy—"rolled round in earth's diurnal course", passive, insentient, like the rocks and stones and trees. The switch from subjective to objective, and from life to death, is the more powerful for being made without warning, undemonstratively.

Compare that poem with the military metaphor in the last section but one of Bishop King's *The Exequy:* his wife has died untimely:

> *'Tis true, with shame and grief I yield*
> *Thou like the van first took'st the field,*
> *And gotten hast the victory*
> *In thus adventuring to die*
> *Before me, whose more years might crave*
> *A just precedence in the grave.*

But hark! My pulse like a soft drum
Beats my approach, tells thee I come;
And slow howe'er my marches be,
I shall at last sit down by thee.

The Exequy is a fine poem; and it carries a weight of emotion no less than that of 'A slumber did my spirit seal'. But it is explicit in a way the Wordsworth poem is not: and we are aware of the poet's ingenuity *playing* over his bereavement. This serious intellectual play limits the poem's imaginative resonance, even in "My pulse like a soft drum/Beats my approach". Metaphysical metaphor always gives me the impression of a fingernail striking a glass and the finger at once laid on the glass's rim to stop the resonance; whereas in romantic metaphor the tone goes ringing on.

The Wordsworth poem points to another resource tapped by lyrical verse. Apart from 'diurnal', its words are quite ordinary—a selection of the language really used by men: no poeticism, only two slight inversions of the natural word-order. Donne, of course, made brilliant use of colloquialism. But it is not till Wordsworth that we find the prospect opening up of poets' using in *lyrical* verse the movement of common speech. This could not be done while the lyric was enthralled to music, which demanded a smoother, more regular surface. As the principle of genre faded out, and lyrical poetry enlarged its scope, poets could loosen up their language, break away from poetic forms and diction which were appropriate to musical interpretation. The singing line could be broadened by an alliance with the speaking line: it was, and still is, a fascinating technical problem—how to incorporate some of the roughness, flexibility and down-to-earthness of common idiom into a lyrical texture. Browning, Emily Dickinson, and Hardy, Yeats in his late lyrics, Edward Thomas and Robert Frost, have diversely solved this problem. But we can find the lyrical-colloquial blend as far back as Keats.

The first two stanzas of 'In a drear-nighted December' are
pure lyric. The winter tree is happy, not remembering its
'green fertility': the frozen brook does not remember its
summer bubblings. But then the poet modulates into this:

Ah! would 'twere so with many
A gentle girl and boy!
But were there ever any
Writh'd not at passèd joy?
The feel of not to feel it,
When none there is to heal it,
Nor numbèd sense to steal it,
Was never said in rhyme.

That stanza is nearer to the run of common speech, while
maintaining the lyrical movement. And its fifth line—which
I greatly prefer to the variant most editors print, "To know
the change and feel it"—has a colloquial naïveté and an
intimate flavour which make it stand up wonderfully well to
the responsibility of being a key-line, the beginning of the
poem's resolution. Here too is the predominant attitude of
nineteenth-century lyrical writing towards the past—one of
regret, and nostalgia: a sixteenth- or seventeenth-century
lyricist, faced with the transience of things, was likely to put
a brave face on it, to treat it briskly, casually, gaily even—
"Gather ye rosebuds while ye may": "Go lovely rose—/Tell
her that wastes her time and me" . . .

Yet another effect of the liberation of poetry from music
is, paradoxically, a nostalgic yearning for the partner it has
lost. This leads to what we sometimes call 'pure poetry':
certain lyrics of Beddoes, for instance, are quite surrealist in
tone—"Old Adam, the carrion crow" or "We do lie beneath
the grass": we think of poems by Poe and Swinburne, where
sense is entirely subordinate to verbal music. Carried to its
lyrical (and quite permissible) conclusion, this development
of the lyric brings us on one hand to the nonsense poems of

Lear, on the other to the poetry of Mallarmé which, as Dr. Elizabeth Sewell has said, "is so pure that it is about poetry and nothing else at all, a form commenting on a form, the content irrelevant."

The purity of Mallarmé is by no means similar to that of Wallace Stevens: but they are infinitely closer to each other than they are to the purity of English and French lyric-writing in the sixteenth century. Poe wanted poems to be *all* poetry, not islands of poetry linked by seas of mere verse. This meant that connection must go. The modern poet who follows this line must, so to say, burn his bridges: Eliot and Pound have little use for bridge-passages. And it is the same with the innovating modern composer: Webern avoids connection because he seeks to avoid the known, and the result in his music is "a banishing of melody". Melody— a singing *line*—has always been essential to the lyric and the lyrical poem as we know them. When poets and composers are impelled to break this line, to give us the pearls without the string, at least to order words or notes in systems of progression which constitute, as it were, a closed circuit, a purely formal relationship, what becomes of the lyric impulse?

If some lyrical writing has aspired to the condition of music, some literary criticism of recent years has aspired to the condition of science. This aspiration tempts certain critics into the supercilious or brash bumptiousness of tone, the complacence, the lack of humility, which can be heard in the utterances of the more mediocre nineteenth-century scientists. But what is to the point in the present context is the effect of our critical climate upon the lyric impulse. Irony, toughness, ambiguity—these are qualities the modern critic can get his teeth into; poems which contain them exercise his full resources. Upon the lyric, smoother, purer,

simpler, he finds it difficult to get a purchase. Faced with
'O wert thou in the cauld blast' or

> *He came all so still*
> *Where his mother was,*
> *As dew in April*
> *That falleth on the grass*

what on earth can the critic say that will not diminish the
poem's effect by officiously enlarging upon it? He would do
best to give it a silent nod and step out of the light: but
critics are a voluble tribe, to whom silence does not come
easily. One can well understand why they direct our attention to the less pure, more complex kinds of poetry where
their guidance can be of great value. One may also suspect
that the emphasis their criticism throws upon such poetry
has contributed to the present decline of interest in the lyric.

But there are causes far more important than the critical
climate for this coldness towards lyric. I have already suggested one or two. That nightingale, for instance: how can
we be lyrical about its song, now we know its cause to be
the bird's digestive process? Well, I don't think this should
inhibit us. After all, few poets who have ever listened to a
nightingale seem to have heard it: what they heard was a
myth. The nightingale's song is neither plaintive nor melancholy: it is exuberant, extrovert, aggressive, But Keats' *Ode*
does not aim to be a contribution to ornithology: he is concerned with the states of mind which a nightingale's song
set going in him, and what sets them going is not the
physical quality of the song but the myth of Philomela. Or
take those objects so assiduously celebrated by the Elizabethan lyricist—his lady's eyes. Would he have praised them
less, or differently, had he known them to be bits of jelly
each of which contains 'about 137 million "seeing" elements
spread out on the sheet of the retina'? He would not: the
information is amazing, but not to his purpose. He probably

possessed enough anatomical learning to know that the beautiful creature was a bag of bones, intestines, blood and water.
But why should this inhibit him? He wants to give the girl
pleasure and tell the world what a wonder she is: he's a poet,
not an anatomist. The lyric poet must try to tell the truth,
yes, but not the whole truth and nothing but the truth.

It is here that the question of sincerity comes up. 'Sincerity' was a watchword of the English 'Movement' poets in
the Fifties: suspicious of shapeless enthusiasm and uncon-
trolled exuberance, they required that a poet should say no
more than he means. This discipline, combined with their
insistence upon the technical rigours of form, was a valuable
corrective to the wild and whirling sort of rhetoric against
which they were reacting; but it also produced a great deal
of dull, correct, low-pressure verse. It may be right for a poet
to say no more than he sincerely means; but a *poem* which
says no more to us than the poet thought he meant is unlikely to be a lasting poem or even a very good one. Sincerity
is an active virtue only in personal poems (Dr. Leavis
brought this out admirably in his discussion of Hardy's "After
a Journey"): we should never think of using the word about
Homer or Shakespeare, Dante or Milton.

Once a poet begins thinking in terms of sincerity, he lays
himself open to that self-consciousness which clogs the
springs of the lyric impulse. If it is more difficult now to write
a simple poem in praise of nature because we know too
much about nature's mechanism, so it must be more difficult
to write a simple love poem:—do I *really* feel as much about
her as I want to say I feel? is she *really* so beautiful, graceful,
charming, mysterious, as I make her out to be? When a poet
loses his nerve in this sense, begins measuring and hedging,
he may write an excellent poem but it will not be a lyric.
Yet, although his feelings about the beloved will illude him
into believing her a nonpareil, the lyrical poet must have the

courage of these illusions or else deny the power of his feelings.

It is the same with another kind of love-poetry—poems in praise of famous men, heroic poetry. We did not need Freud to tell us that the springs of action are impure, or that no one has ever been wholly and always admirable. The poet's capacity for wonder and reverence can be directed, as Yeats showed often enough, not upon a character for whom he deceives himself into total hero-worship, whose motives and actions he consistently admires, but upon the quality of a given action—what Hopkins called 'Honour flashed off exploit'. It was the quintessence of man or woman, as revealed in action, which drew from Yeats the impulse of lyrical praise and justified him in it: 'Easter 1916' is at once an absolutely honest poem and an exaltation of the terrible beauty which the Easter Rising gave birth to. This free yielding-up of oneself—it may be to a person, an event, or a cause—is surely a poetic virtue whose loss would be crippling to us. As Sir Osbert Sitwell said about the young Wilfrid Owen, "He manifested a tremendous capacity for admiration, for reverence: a quality which perhaps every poet, however much of a rebel he may be in other directions, must needs possess."

Civilised man's increasing self-consciousness, and the displacement of a mythological view of nature by a scientific one, have certainly made fine lyric-writing a difficult matter today for any poet who cannot accept the principles of Mallarmé or the practice of the surrealists. Ideally, he would like to marry the animism which appeals to his heart with the scientific view which convinces his head, but it is an almost impossible marriage. Theoretically, a poet should be able to exclude from his mind the theory, say, of an expanding universe while writing a lyric in which the stars are an image of steadfastness or of hope or of his mistress' eyes: but

in practice the scientific view will keep nagging at him, com-
plicating the issue, demanding recognition: he cannot revert
to the relative unsophistication of his ancestors without feeling that he has falsified modern knowledge or failed it: he
cannot include such knowledge and write a simple lyric
poem, since scientific data and theory, until they have been
thoroughly assimilated by the general imagination—until,
that is to say, an allusion to them is as readily accepted by the
common reader as an allusion to Prometheus or Puck—cannot be tuned in with a lyric utterance.

This is one of the most awkward dilemmas facing the poet
today. But the gravest problem of all arises from language.
The world is being rapidly overpopulated by the word.
Wherever we move, we are assailed or solicited by words,
spewing out at us from the presses, deafening us from radio
and television. Can you wonder that in this almighty shindy
the lyric utterance, which is a still, small voice, goes unheard,
or that lyrical poets should be tempted into straining their
voices in order to be heard? It is one of the poet's tasks, as
we know, to purify the language of the tribe: but the task
may well seem hopeless when the poet is confronted by
this Augean stable—the gobbledygook of technologists and
critics, the pompous yet repellently servile idiom of business
correspondence, the reach-me-down, utility style of most
newspapers, the weird jargon concocted by civil servants, and
worst of all, the hectic flush imparted to language by publicists and advertisers. The bogus floweriness of the latter, the
barbarous, pretentious, or complacently drab tones of the
others, are enough to make poetry despair. Poetry's language
should be a heightening of the common language; but, when
so much of that language is either vile or without flavour,
the poet has no sound basis from which to work.

He may try to shout down the general pandemonium, as
Dylan Thomas did, by sheer weight and eccentricity of lan-

guage. The same effort can be seen in much American verse of the last forty years. Vigorous and adventurous though it is, the reader cannot help noticing how desperately words are often strained, dislocated even, in order to get away from cliché and give an appearance of 'originality'. This distortion of language, whether it comes from complexity of thought or from a craving for novelty, goes counter to the lyric impulse, which is for simplicity both in words and in thought. The good lyrics of the past flowered, after all, from emotional commonplaces: today, when advertisers consult psychologists as to how best they may work emotively upon their prospective customers, a giant crop of clichés, like vivid and poisonous weeds, encroaching upon the field of lyric, has impoverished its soil.

It would be difficult to overestimate the harm done to language by modern advertisement. Amongst other things, the flowery, cynical appeals of publicists have set up a strong but undiscriminating reaction. If a man speaks eloquently, with panache, we at once suspect him of insincerity: we feel he is trying to get at us. This attitude of ours has spread over into literature. To many critics and younger writers in Britain, 'charm', 'grace', 'style' are naughty words: 'style'— yet every writer must have a style of some sort—is equated with superficiality or exhibitionism, all manner and no matter. Here again the lyric suffers. A lyric poem must have some sort of grace; and charm is, after all, *carmen*—a lyric song. If we so distrust charm and grace and style, and will have nothing but honest, rugged poetry with no nonsense about it, we are discouraging the lyric impulse, and in doing so we cut off the main stream of poetry from one of its tributaries.

The demand for sincerity, to return to it once more, in so far as it means that a poem should not say phony things, is simply a demand that the poem should be good: well, we heartily agree. In so far as it means a banning of the flamboyant, the exorbitant, the passionate or the pretty, it clearly won't do. The truth of poetry is a truth which transcends sincerity, and disposes or suppresses facts for its own purpose. It has nothing to do with the equally valid but prose truth of science. And this is so over the whole range of poetry, from 'The moving moon went up the sky' to 'the moving toyshop of the heart'. But especially it is so for lyric and lyrical poetry; the lyric impulse, when it possesses a poet, asks one thing of him above all, a pure commitment without reserve or circumspection to the creature of his love.

2. WORDS AND MUSIC

"No songless people has ever been discovered," says the *Oxford Companion to Music*; and it goes on to tell us that only men and birds sing, not animals. This is not quite true: I myself sang last year to a seal on the west coast of Scotland, and it replied to me, with a strangulated but unmistakably melodious kind of mooing. I am satisfied that the animal (or is it a fish?) was at least making a passionate attempt to sing, to break out from inarticulateness. We imagine human song originating in rhythmic, wordless sounds to accompany a dance; a painful effort to be articulate, to express and heighten the communal feeling realised in the dance; a means of communicating. And at last the sounds became words. And so began the ever-recurrent conflict between poet and musician. They should be equal partners; but there have been few times when either words or music did not have the upper hand—at least in principle.

In the Odes of Pindar, say, or Bacchylides, there is no doubt that music held the subordinate position. In the choruses of Handelian opera, to go to the other extreme, the words (often very nice words) seem little more than pegs on which to hang the music. What the poet complains of is that the composer plays havoc with his poem, altering its rhythms, dwelling upon the least important words, repeating phrases that were not meant to be repeated, falsifying the poem's formal values. The composer, on the other hand— well, listen to Mozart:

Why, an opera is sure of success when the plot is well worked out, the words written solely for the music and not shoved in here and there to suit some miserable rhyme . . . Verses are indeed the most indispensable element for music—but rhymes—solely for the sake of rhyming—the most detrimental . . . Poets almost remind me of trumpeters with their professional tricks! If we composers were always to stick so faithfully to our rules . . . we should be concocting music as unpalatable as their libretti.

With opera, of course, it is accepted that the musician should take first place. But Mozart's complaint about the egotism and intransigence of poets is echoed by many composers of other kinds of vocal music. In the same letter Mozart says,

The best thing of all is when a good composer who understands the stage and is talented enough to make sound suggestions, meets an able poet, that true phoenix . . .

Such a collaboration of equals, so necessary for opera (the Purcell-Dryden partnership is pre-eminent in Britain), can apply no less to the writers of lyric song, as the great age of the Lutanists proved.

We may take up here Mozart's strictures on rhyme, because they lead into the heart of our subject—what is the special nature of words for music? In every language there are certain poetic measures which music finds unamenable: in English, the heroic couplet is the most obvious of these. Though he was a defender of rhyme, Samuel Daniel declared heroic couplets to be "very tiresome and unpleasing, by reason that . . . they run on with a sound of one nature, and with a kind of certainty which stuffs the delight rather than entertains it." Daniel is not specifically concerned here with words for music. But he put his finger upon the reason why composers have fought shy of the heroic couplet: it is too regular, too monotonous, and the lines are too long: what Elizabethan composers liked best were metres in which five-beat lines are mixed with shorter ones and perhaps an occasional longer one. What repelled them about the heroic couplet was, in fact, its lack of metrical variety. The iambic pentameter, which Campion gave reasons for considering the English equivalent of the classical hexameter, though it could be handled with the contrapuntal technique of the madrigalist, was almost impossible for the writer of solo airs to manage without distortion of the poetic rhythms.

The genius of a language, in relation to music, is an elusive thing. For example, Virgil wrote the singing-matches of the *Eclogues* in the same hexameters as he used for the poems in which they are placed. It is possible that a Roman reader, accepting the convention, might have heard these passages as song—heard rhythmical subtleties which created for him the illusion of men singing. The same impression could not possibly be given in English. So, when I translated the *Eclogues*, I kept the body of the text in six-beat lines, but used English and Irish folk-song metres for the singing-matches.

In Italy and France, the sonnet was a piece to be sung. When it came to England, the different genius of our language set obstacles in the way of composers. Sonnets, and other short poems in regular five-beat metre, demanded a special treatment. Below is the first stanza of Dowland's 'Come, heavy sleep':

Come heavy Sleep, the image of true Death,
And close up these—my weary weeping eyes
Whose spring of tears doth stop my vital breath,
And tears my heart with Sorrow's sigh-swoln cries.
Come and possess my tired thought-worn soul,
That living dies, till thou on me be stole.

Hearing it sung, the ear simply cannot take in that this poem
was written in regular five-beat lines. Dowland has had to
wrench the metre out of recognition and impose quite different musical rhythms upon it.

And we cannot ascribe such distortion merely to the
musical idiom of Dowland's time. For example,

Your hands lie open in the long fresh grass,
The finger points look through like rosy blooms:
*Your eyes smile peace.**

These are the opening lines of a D. G. Rossetti sonnet, set
by Vaughan Williams, a composer who usually kept close
to the rhythmic values of a poem he was setting. To make
a song of this sonnet, although he did not distort the values
of the individual words, he had to evolve music in which
the poem's overall metre is quite lost.

Contrast with those two examples Purcell's setting, below,
of Dryden's 'Fairest Isle, all isles excelling'.

* From "Silent Noon" by Daniel Gabriel Rossetti in *The House of Life.*
Lyric and music are reprinted here with permission, respectively, of Edwin
Ashdon Ltd. and Mrs. Ralph Vaughan Williams.

Fairest Isle, all Isles excelling
Seat of pleasures and of loves,
Venus here will choose her dwelling,
And forsake her Cyprian groves.

Cupid from his fav'rite nation
Care and envy will remove,
Jealousy that poisons passion,
And despair that dies for love.

Although Purcell, using a sarabande rhythm, introduces much decoration, and puts emphasis on unimportant words or on syllables we would not stress in reading the poem, our ear never loses its rapid, regular four-beat metre.

Dowland's distortion of the pentameter is justified by Mr. Peter Pears in these terms:—

His way with words could seem arbitrary to those accustomed to the practice of song-writers since, from Purcell to Britten. The clue to this strange emphasis lies in the great weight Dowland gives to the line of the voice. In all these big songs of his the voice is one of the strands of counterpoint—the most important— of which the song is made.[1]

Dowland, in effect, was using the voice as a leading instrument, and foreshadowing thus the great advances made by instrumental chamber music later in the seventeenth century.

During the lutanist period, the vast preponderance of English music was vocal. The poet looked to music as "the natural comrade and illustration of his own art": and, as William Byrd wrote, "The music should be framed to the life of the words". But we must remember too that poets, Campion, for instance, who called his own lyrics "ear-pleasing rhymes, without art," considered the lyric—words for music—as a genre inferior to other kinds of poetry because more restricted, not autonomous. The most obvious of these restrictions was, quite simply, the need for the words to be audible (a need not invariably satisfied by later composers). During the great song-writing period of 1560–1620, composers do seem to have been at one with poets in honouring this need: Mr. John Stevens[2] has suggested that this happy state of affairs was brought about by the Reformation, which encouraged men to read the Bible and in general to feel a greater respect for words. In this context we may remember Erasmus' diatribe against monks in 1516:—"A set of creatures who ought to be lamenting their sins fancy they can please God by gurgling in their throats": he is attacking the polyphony of the early Tudor church, which was not concerned to put over the meaning of the words it sung.

Not only did composers of the great period take trouble to render the words of their songs audible: they also introduced an expressiveness seldom heard before—a music related to the emotions of the poems they were setting, as music had not previously been related except in certain kinds of folk-song. With the modal rhythm of the Middle Ages, we find that the words were used to give the measure of the notes: this music did not attempt to 'express' the meaning of the text; and it was the singer's task, rather than the poet's, to fit the words to the notes. As late as the fifteenth century, the relationship between poetry and music does not enter rhetorical theory at all. Mr. Stevens argues that only in folk-song was there a natural, un-selfconscious union between words and tune: in other music, their marriage was a marriage of convenience—and one which broke up when, after the thirteenth century, music was increasingly able to stand on its own feet.

The 1560–1620 period saw a reunion: a reunion on an altogether higher plane of musical accomplishment. It was now that English composers began to interpret through their music the moods of poems. By means of varying tempi, of interval, phrasing and cadence, both madrigalists and lutanist composers sought to express the emotional content (some madrigals are almost programme-music in the way they reproduce a poem's meanings, and madrigal-writers tried hard to follow the verbal rhythms of a poem in the several parts); till we come to the great songs of Dowland— "works of tremendous power," as Professor Bruce Pattison puts it, "in which the emotions of the poetry seem to dictate their own form."[3]

But even now the writer of words for music had to work within a narrow compass. It is true that music and poetry are both temporal arts, throwing the attention always forward. But in reading a poem one can stop and look back, whereas in hearing a song one must be carried along with the music or else stop listening altogether. So the emotions which the poem gave the musician to express had to be simple emotions, and its language un-obscure: the poet would have been ill-advised to offer the audience subtle or complex phrases which a listener would need to think over and so lose the musical thread. What the Elizabethan composer wanted from a poem was consistency of tone together with metrical variety; and the lyric writer gave it to him. To quote Professor Pattison again,

Sixteenth-century poets . . . did not attempt effects that would not be appreciated by the listener or for which the composer would have difficulty in creating suitable music.[4]

It was a period, as we know, when music was everywhere: not only the lute and virginals at home, but the cittern hanging in the barber's shop; not only the musical party in the great house, but apprentices, journeymen, peasants, street vendors singing at their work, and Sir Francis Drake taking a band on one of his voyages to show foreigners what a musical people the English were. Moreover, as I have said earlier, there was no hostility between popular song and the art of professionals or Court amateurs. Marlowe had written 'Come, live with me,' to a traditional ballad tune: Raleigh and Donne wrote variants of the poem intended, we can reasonably assume, for the same air. Sidney composed words for the famous tune of 'Greensleeves'. The printers of broadside ballads, to be sold among the common people, did not exclude poems written by good poets.

But towards the end of this period the fruitful relationship between lyricist and composer grew thinner: each began to strain away from the other. From the poet's point of view, the strict patterning necessary for a poem to be set to music, the need for every line to be end-stopped so as to provide the composer with a cadence, the need for exact strophic form—all this, which had at first stimulated his art, now began to cramp it. The freer use of speech-rhythms counterpointing the metre in Jacobean drama must have made poets intolerant of the absolutism of metre imposed by song lyric. Because of its strict pattern and conventional content, poetry written for music is monotonous to read; and the printed page was supplanting the voice as the chief medium of poetry. Though Donne was fond of music, and expected musical setting for his *Songs and Sonnets*, the quality of metaphysical verse demanded reading. And, as

the seventeenth century advanced, to quote Professor Pattison again,

Though poets were still knowledgeable about music, it was the
result of social contacts rather than any close ties between the
two arts. The gulf between them was widening. Poetry was
exploiting speech rythm, and music was perfecting its own formal
principles. Both were following the inner necessities of their own
natures.[5]

Let us now try to look more closely at the nature of words
for music. I have said elsewhere that they are like water-
weed which only comes alive in its natural element: separated from it—from music—they look dead, without lustre
or movement. This is put, rather more professionally, by
V. C. Clinton-Baddeley in his admirable book on the subject:[6]

Words for music are incomplete words. They represent, and
are intended to represent, an incomplete thought. The finished
words of a song are only half a song. Within the limits of its
technique the words can attain perfection—but it is the essential
quality of that technique that the words presuppose, demand,
and await the addition of music.

This is a downright statement. We must except from it
poems which were not written for music but have been given
musical settings: poems which invite composers, such as A.
E. Housman's, or Hardy's 'To Lizbie Brown' which the late
Gerald Finzi set so beautifully; and poems one would never
associate with music at all until a composer finds in them
what he needs—I am thinking particularly of Benjamin
Britten's magnificent use of certain Wilfrid Owen poems in
his *War Requiem.*

Keeping to poems actually written for music, we must ask
ourselves to what extent Mr. Clinton-Baddeley is right in
saying "they represent, and are intended to represent, an
incomplete thought." It is a tempting idea; but the trouble
is that the 'thought' of music is different from the 'thought'

of poetry. We cannot conceive of a poet deliberately writing a poem with, so to speak, a hole in it which the composer is to fill up. The composer can only 'complete' the poem's thought in the sense of interpreting its moods. "The intellectual appeal of music," writes Professor Pattison, "is quite different from that of poetry. It is more related to structure than to content. The 'thought' of poetry has no parallel in music. The two arts can meet only on an emotional plane."[7]

Nevertheless, if we substitute for 'thought' some vaguer word like 'being' or 'existence', we may accept Mr. Clinton-Baddeley's statement. To put it at its simplest, with words written for a pre-existing tune, or words for which a now familiar tune was written—'Auld Lang Syne', for example, or 'Drink to me only' or 'Land of Hope and Glory'—it is the tune which we have uppermost in our heads (unless we are tone-deaf) and which reminds us of the words. Or again, how difficult it is to *read aloud* a poem such as 'As Fond Kiss' or Blake's 'Jerusalem', if we know it in the context of a familiar melody: we want to sing it: the musical phrasing overshadows the verbal phrasing, although 'Jerusalem' and 'As Fond Kiss' are excellent poems in their own right.

Where such works are concerned, the music obviously is—or has become—the senior partner. Almost every composer needs to alter the verbal values of a lyric if he is to make a song of it. Is there any poet who has altered the musical values of a tune in order to adapt it to his own words? I can only think of Thomas Moore, who changed many notes in the Irish folk-airs, and often slowed down the tempi of traditional dance-tunes; he did so because his age demanded that a poem should be regular, so that "the irregular structure of many of those airs, and the lawless kind of metre," as he put it, had to be tamed. The Elizabethan lyricist would put into a poem a refrain which its sense did not require, simply as a convenience for the music; and if he did not, the composer was quite capable of putting in a verbal refrain himself. I myself, as a poet, would not reject on principle the composer's right to take liberties with my text, any more than, if I were a novelist, I should resent the alterations a script-writer and a director must make in my novel to create a good movie from it. The novel, the poem, are still *there* in the original form, intact on paper: the movie, the song, are new objects of art, and like any other translations must be judged primarily by the standards of the language into which they are translated, whether cinematic or musical.

Was it not Yeats' lack of musical training which caused him to write these strictures?

> Music that wants of us nothing but images that suggest sound, cannot be our music . . . such music can but dislocate, wherever there is syntax and elaborate rhythm. The poet, his ear attentive to his own art, hears with derision most settings of his work . . . And yet there are old songs that melt him into tears.[8]

One understands Yeats' objection. There is a story that George Moore met him one afternoon near the Albert Hall, and asked him why he looked so distraught. "Moore," said Yeats, "I have just heard my poem, 'The Lake Isle of Innisfree', sung by a choir of ten thousand Boy Scouts." But there were old songs that melted him into tears: one of these, 'The Rambling Boys of Pleasure', he turned into a lyric as elegant and musical as any of Tom Moore's—'Down by the Sally Gardens'.

The points I wish to make are two and quite simple. First, if a poet is moved to write words for a tune he likes, he should at least know enough about singing to place his vowels conveniently for the voice, to avoid awkward clashes of consonants, to write in phrases which are not beyond a singer's powers of breathing, and in general to use the tune as a technical and an emotional guide. Thomas Moore, otherwise an inconsiderable poet, was a master of song-writing because he understood the singer's technical needs. Writers who compose a vaguely lyrical poem and entitle it 'Song', as too many do nowadays (and Wordsworth did twice), are making nonsense of the idea of lyric. Secondly, if the poet writes words for a composer, or words which a composer lights upon as material for a song, he must allow the composer to take charge, not expecting his own rhythms to be reproduced, not thinking of musical notes as a mere underlining or heightening of his poetic texture.

Just as a familiar tune may call forth words from a poet, so words may challenge a composer. It is the recalcitrance of a poem, I suggest, that first interests him: if he merely wanted vocal noises for his music, he would write music giving the voice a series of meaningless sounds such as we find in Hebridean 'mouth-music'. Why struggle to translate a poem into the language of music, when you could by-pass the problem through the use of vocal sounds that have no intellectual sense? through employing the voice as a solo instrument? The answer, surely, is that a poem—meaningful sound—gives the composer musical ideas which nonsense-sound will not give him: the foreignness of words sets up in his mind that friction from which thematic sparks may fly. Mouth-music is a throwback to the days before language, when a dance was accompanied by rhythmic vocal noises. The composer cannot regress to this medium, except occasionally for the purpose of such atmospheric effects as Vaughan Williams aimed at in the 1st and 5th movements of his *Antarctica Symphony*.

Just how a poem inspires a musical idea, I have no notion —any more than I can explain why one experience will lead to a poem and another will not. The poetic quality of the lyric seems to have no say in the matter at all. Wolf chose good poems on the whole: Benjamin Britten, in his *Serenade for Tenor and Horn*, for instance, his *Spring Symphony* or his *Nocturne*, has shown an extraordinary flair for using good poems that seem to bear no relation to one another till he constellates them into a musical sequence. But the greatest of all song-writers, Schubert, for the most part used quite mediocre poems. Is it just that Schubert had bad taste in verse? Or is it that his particular genius needed words which had nothing to commend them but a conventional lyric mellifluousness? poems which, lacking any depth or originality of meaning, evoked his own creative power to supply what they lacked? Certainly *his* choice of poems bears out the argument that words for music must be incomplete. But when Mr. Clinton-Baddeley states, of the Housman poem beginning—

> *That is the land of lost content,*
> *I see it shining plain,*
> *The happy highways where I went*
> *And cannot come again.*[9]

—"It is not possible to write music for words like these without disturbing their balance and quenching their sincerity,"[10] I must firmly dissent. To me, though it is a complete poem, it does also seem to be asking for music.

Lyrical poetry, as I have said, has never quite lost touch with its origin in music. An instance of this is the continued use of refrain long after its musical purpose disappeared. In folk-poetry, the refrain was at first uttered by the group, after a solo singer had uttered the stanza: this gave the soloist a breathing-space to recollect, or invent, what should come next. The refrain was a form of what we now call 'audience participation'. It may possibly link us back to early mediaeval dances, where, as Mr. Pattison tells us, "the ring of dancers moved right or left while singing the refrain, and made some sort of marking-time gesture while the soloist sang his part."[11] The Elizabethan composer used a refrain, which the poet put at his disposal or which he inserted himself, as the musical climax to a stanza, or as a coda, knowing that it would give the ear a double pleasure of recognition when it heard the same musical and verbal phrase repeated. Audience participation again, though of a more passive nature. The refrain could be a generalised pointing of the sense of the poem as a whole; or it could be the 'hey-nonny-no' type of non-sense, which gave the composer absolute freedom of interpretation.

Repetition of some kind is integral to poetry. Rhyme is a form of it: so is alliteration: so are the balanced reiterations we hear in the Psalms, and the balanced antitheses of Pope: so is the image which reminds us of an earlier image in the poem. But refrain is the form of repetition special to lyric poetry, whether it comes in story-lyrics (ballads), in popular song, or in art-songs. We can have the simple chorus-refrain, like Sheridan's "Let the toast pass,/Drink to the lass,/I'll warrant she'll prove an excuse for the glass": the nonsense refrain, like "Toroddle toroddle, toroll," in Goldsmith's 'The Three Pigeons'. And there is the more indirect refrain we get in Tennyson's 'song' from *The Princess*, which begins each stanza with 'now' followed by a verb ("Now sleeps the crimson petal" . . . "Now droops" . . . "Now lies" . . . "Now slides" . . . "Now folds"); and each stanza ends with 'me' ("waken thou with me" . . . "glimmers on to me" . . . "open unto me" . . . "thy thoughts in me" . . . "Is lost in me"). The same type of echo refrain is heard in a familiar poem by Christina Rosetti, but here each line in the second stanza gives a counter-echo to the corresponding line of stanza one:

Oh roses for the flush of youth,
   And laurel for the perfect prime;
But pluck an ivy branch for me
   Grown old before my time.

Oh violets for the grave of youth,
   And bay for those dead in their prime;
Give me the withered leaves I chose
   Before in the old time.

Modern use of strict refrain, because the poems were not written with a musical intention, generally strikes my ear as anachronistic, or artificial in the bad sense. I do not like D. G. Rossetti's refrains in 'Sister Helen', 'Troy Town', or 'Eden Bower', for instance; but then I don't like the poems either. Yeats is another matter. He sometimes uses refrain-lines in the traditional way, as a sort of chorus. But in other poems the refrain seems more integral to the poem's meaning, or even to be its key-passage: an example of this is "Like a long-legged fly upon the stream / His mind moves upon silence."[12] In the sequence he provocatively entitled *Words for Music Perhaps*, we find one 'fol-de-rol' refrain, one or two rather perfunctory ones, several which offer gnomic comments upon the stanzas and perhaps carry a shade too much weight of meaning—at any rate, if we expect a refrain to be hypnotic rather than to set us worrying what its symbolism stands for: but we also find one superb refrain-line, 'Mad as the mist and snow', which without any riddling adds great force to each of the three stanzas and takes a slightly different colour from each.

Strict refrain is an echo, signalling the end of a stanza, rounding things off neatly, recalling the closed or cyclic form of the lyric. But there are other kinds of echoing, as we have seen. "How sweet the answer" is one of Tom Moore's less-known but most graceful songs: it is a pattern of echoes, a poem without guile, unpretentious and delicate; and it modulates with great tact from the lightness of the first two stanzas into the heart-felt resolution of the theme in stanza three:

How sweet the answer Echo makes
  To Music at night,
When, rous'd by lute or horn, she wakes,
And, far away, o'er lawns and lakes,
  Goes answering light!

Yet love hath echoes truer far,
  And far more sweet,
Than e'er beneath the moonlight's star,
Of horn, or lute, or soft guitar,
  The songs repeat.

'Tis when the sigh, in youth sincere,
  And only then,—
The sigh that's breath'd for one to hear,
Is by that one, that only dear,
  Breath'd back again.

The lilt of 'To Music at night' and 'Goes answering light' is not repeated elsewhere in the words; but it is imparted to them throughout by the air—a dancing tune called 'The Wren', so that, although the verbal metre is iambic, the musical one plays iambic off against triplets. These lilting measures came into English poetry through the influence of dance music at Court, when the stately dances of Elizabeth and James gave way to livelier ones, the saraband, volta, and coranto. Charles II was particularly fond of the French dance music of his time, and poets were still in close enough touch with music to be affected by musical developments. Davenant's play, *The Law Against Lovers*, first acted in 1662, contains the song 'Wake all the dead', which plays iambs against dactyls—

> *Wake all the dead! what ho! what ho!*
> *How soundly they sleep whose pillows lie low!*
> *They mind not poor lovers who walk above*
> *On the decks of the world in storms of love . . .*

Some of the songs in Dryden's plays were written for triple time, and are dactylic throughout—"After the pangs of a desperate lover", for instance, or "Sylvia the fair, in the bloom of Fifteen". This rollicking rhythm suited the mood of the Restoration. And it could be adapted to poetry of a deeper resonance, as Dryden showed in

> *All, all of a piece throughout;*
> *Thy chase had a beast in view,*
> *Thy wars brought nothing about,*
> *Thy lovers were all untrue;*
> *'Tis well an old age is out*
> *And time to begin a new.*

"Dryden," said Tom Moore, "has happily described music as being 'inarticulate poetry'; and I have always felt, in adapting words for an expressive air, that I was but bestowing on it the gift of articulation." In this sense we can agree that, just as song lyrics are incomplete without music, so there are many tunes which are incomplete without words. There is little doubt that the craze for Italian opera in the eighteenth century had the effect of making cultivated English people less exigent about the quality of native words-for-music than they had been in the seventeenth. Simplicity, too, was lost —the kind of simplicity we get from the Caroline lyrics, and from Dryden, Gay, Dibdin, Sheridan, when they were writing lyric verse. Cowper complains, writing about the ballad, "Simplicity and ease are its proper characteristics. Our forefathers excelled in it; but we moderns have lost the art." I do not want to broach the question, how far was the 'simplicity' of the old ballad-writers a matter of naïveté, of not being *able* to write in a more sophisticated, complex way: in any case, simplicity was soon to reappear—though not just the kind which Cowper meant—with the Lyrical Ballads of Wordsworth and Coleridge. What I would like to open, and end with, is the problem of writing simple poems when the close cooperation between poet and composer has been lost, except in the writing of opera.

I would suggest in the first place that dialect is a help. The Dorset dialect poems of William Barnes, who was roughly contemporary with Tennyson, are simple in a manner that Tennyson's lyrics are not; and they are superior to the lyrics which Barnes himself wrote in ordinary English. On this score, he reminds one of Robert Burns, whose literary-English poems are greatly inferior to those he wrote in Scots vernacular. And so one would expect, for Burns was a Scottish countryman of quite humble birth. But Barnes was a schoolmaster, a clergyman, and a considerable philologist; we should not have expected dialect to be the natural medium for such a poet. Yet his Dorset poems are not artificial—they do not in the least give one the impression of an eminent philologist doing poetic exercises in a quaint old dialect. I can only think that, by writing in their language, Barnes tapped the Dorset countryman's simpleness of mind and drew from it the sturdiness and innocence which give his dialect poetry its specific charm. I shall have more to say of him later.

Another interesting case is Lallans. Now this is not a regional form of Scots, nor was it ever the language of real men: it is a literary language both eclectic and artificial. Yet a number of poems—love poems, particularly—have been written in Lallans by modern Scottish poets, which to my ear carry the note of simplicity I am listening for, the lyric purity. If they could be translated into English, or even into contemporary Scots, these poems would still be simple, but with the simpleness of mere banality, I suspect. It really is very odd that poets should have to use a highly artificial, literary language in order to produce an effect of simplicity: but it happens; and it happens, I suppose, because to the ignorant Sassenach reader, at any rate, Lallans gives the feel of a living dialect.

To put it another way, the contemporary poet finds it almost impossible to be simple *naturally*. The lyric seems to him a used-up medium, offering no scope either for the innovation in language or the complexity of thought, one or both of which he seeks to pursue. He may, of course, write off the lyric completely and devote himself to lyrical or pseudo-lyrical poetry. But he may wish to recapture the innocence of the lyric, while not committing himself to 'pure poetry'—a form merely commenting on a form. And it is here that we return to music: music provides, as it were, a cover for simplicity of words, and justifies it: a lyric, which would look nakedly banal in cold print, clothed by a tune need not feel ashamed of itself.

I am not advocating that our poet should go into collaboration with a composer of musical comedy or light opera, though the discipline might do him no harm. Nor, unless he has the musical understanding of an Auden, could I recommend him to write words for more serious living composers, their work being short on what the novice ear can accept as melody. But there are thousands of good traditional tunes available: let him try putting new words to a few of these—as we have seen, there are respectable precedents for it among poets of the past. He cannot wish himself into falling in love with a tune; but it would be strange if no tune ever called to him, as that of 'Chevy Chase' called to

Philip Sidney, or 'And we'll gang nae mair a-roving' to Byron.

Here I shall take the liberty of offering a few attempts of my own. They are lyrics written for definite tunes. Whether they stand up as poems in cold print, I cannot judge: all I know is that they would not have been written just so— indeed, would not have been written at all—but for the prompting of the tunes. The first of them dates back to the slump and unemployment of the early Thirties, which roused me to write indignant verse about the conditions under which so many of our people had to live. One of these poems was a savage pastiche of 'Come, live with me': here I did not have a tune in my head. Another was written to the familiar tune of a carol, 'Away in a manger': it too is pastiche, using strong echoes of the original words the more effectively, I hoped, to shock readers into the same anger and compassion as I myself felt.

Oh hush thee, my baby,
Thy cradle's in pawn·
No blankets to cover thee
Cold and forlorn.
The stars in the bright sky
Look down and are dumb
At the heir of the ages
Asleep in a slum.

The hooters are blowing,
No heed let him take;
When baby is hungry,
'Tis best not to wake

Thy mother is crying,
Thy dad's on the dole;
Two shillings a week is
The price of a soul.[13]

Without the tune to sweep away my self-consciousness and carry me on, I should never have dared to write words so stark, unsophisticated—and, you may feel, for a poet of my generation, sentimental.

During the Forties, I was singing Tom Moore and Irish folk-songs a good deal. I found one air, 'Dermott', which particularly haunted me. Moore had written words for it, and it is one of those grand, sweeping, cello-like tunes which so often brought the best out of him—'When he who adores thee' is an example. But, for once, Moore had not done his melody justice, so I determined to have a go at it myself. It is of great rhythmical interest, which I decided to follow exactly in the words, giving one syllable to each note throughout. Accompanying the musical score is the first of the three stanzas I wrote for this tune:

Love was once light as air
Brushed over all my thoughts and themes;
Love once seemed kind as air
When the dewfall gleams.
Now he's another thing—
Naked light—oh hard to bear,
Too much discovering
With his noonday beams.[14]

That is not pastiche—of Moore or anyone else. And if you look up Moore's words, 'Take back the virgin page', you will see how a good tune may be open to more than one verbal interpretation: indeed, it should be open to as many as there are poets whom it fastens upon. My own lyric was no more a technical exercise than was the one I wrote for 'Away in a manger': it arose from a certain situation in love, and it was heartfelt. But again, the emotion could never have taken so simple a form of words without the encouragement of a sympathetic tune. The modern poet, writing words for a traditional air, must consult its feelings; and this may mean putting aside his usual bag of tricks for the time being. Violent, obtrusive metaphor, for instance, can well be out of place and quarrel with the tune: in the first two lines of the stanza above, a metaphor from air-brushing, used to touch up a photograph, is so toned down that it virtually disappears into "Love was once light as *air* / *Brushed* over all my thoughts and themes".

Last, let me give a set of words written for the air, 'St. Patrick's Day,—another one used by Moore. Some years before, I had written two lyrics, 'Jig' and 'Hornpipe', based upon the two Irish dance-rhythms but not upon any specific tune. 'St. Patrick's Day' is a dance tune, too, quick and catchy. I approached it more as an exercise, and with none of the personal emotion that went into 'Love was once light as air': such emotion would have taken a tearful toss from a tune so mettlesome and gay, or else crippled it altogether. Its dancing rhythm, like that of 'Jig' and 'Hornpipe', seemed to call for a great complexity of end-rhyme and internal rhyming; and one could supply this without any fear that it might distract from the sense, because the sense would be entirely frivolous anyway. This, together with the rapidity of the rhythm permitted me to mix (as I had done in 'Jig' and 'Hornpipe') a modern reference with traditional ones: the reader will catch a glimpse of Sir James Frazer towards the end of stanza one, before he is whirled away: a song of slower tempo would have given such an allusion the most disagreeable prominence. In short, the lyric is nothing more than a web of rhymes; or the verbal equivalent of what Sir Thomas Beecham called his musical 'lollipops'.

Oh light was my head as the seed of a thistle
And light as the mistletoe mooning an oak,
I spoke with the triton, I skimmed with the nautilus,
Dawn was immortal as love awoke.
    But when a storm began to blow
    My thistle was dashed, my tree laid low,
    My folk of the wave went down to their deep, so I
Frown on a thistledown floating capriciously,
Scorn as mere fishes the folk of the sea,
Agree the renowned golden bough is a parasite,
Love but a gallous-eyed ghost for me.

Ah, fooled by the cock at the cool of the morning
And fooled by the fawning mirage of the day,
I say that I'm truly well rid of this featherwit—
Reason has tethered it down in clay.

But when the light begins to go,
When shadows are marching, heel and toe,
When day is a heap of ashes, I know that I'll
Ride to love's beam like a barque at her anchorage,
Glide on the languorous airs of the past,
For fast as the pride of our reason is waning,
Old follies returning grow wise at last.

The point I am trying to make is that, unless some poets are willing to experiment with words for music, the lyric impulse as it has been felt for centuries may fade out completely, and the lyric tradition be dead. One may feel that this is no great matter: and I am myself deeply suspicious of attempts to revive any art form, such as the Greek dance, which has long outlived its meaning. But there is modern dancing, from twisting to Ballet, to supply our emotional needs whether as spectators or participants: nothing, on the other hand, has turned up to replace lyric—nothing except bad lyrics, or the skilful but fugitive ones of the contemporary musical. Poets today may feel that what they have to say cannot be accommodated by the lyric form, and that any attempt to do so would be putting new wine into old bottles. I sympathise with this; but I'm worried about anything which diminishes the range, the variousness of poetry: epic, narrative, satire, lyrical and lyric—they should all cross-fertilize one another, and the decline of any one must leave the rest poorer.

The closest link, of course, is between lyrical and lyric. As I have said, if we look at American and English poetry today, we see that the great bulk of it consists in the hybrids we call 'lyrical': poems are generally short, and although the 'singing line' has not been altogether discarded, it is constantly being broken by our modern practice of the elliptic —we leave out many links of meaning, so that the final effect is one of violent juxtapositions; and among all these deliberate discords, the tune is apt to get lost. We wish to pack our poems tight, condense their meaning; and as a result there is a sameness about much modern verse—a sort of glumness and opacity—as though poets feel they must at all costs guard their work against charges of frivolity or thinness. I suggest that this dense, concentrated texture of modern poetry needs *aerating*. The lyric poet, to achieve his purity and simplicity, has had to let a lot of air in. I think we can still learn from him.

Association with music can help here. If you write words for a tune, you find the tune clears much of the verbal undergrowth for you. Music may do other things too: the Elizabethan composer encouraged the poet to experiment with lines of different lengths in regular stanzas; we may reasonably see a connection between Thomas Hardy's musical knowledge and the remarkable variety of stanza form we find in his poetry. Today in England young poets are experimenting with poetry and jazz; while the great increase in broadcasts, public recitals, and recordings of verse over the last twenty years has shown that many people enjoy listening to poetry who seldom or never read it. I do not myself think this is an artificial revival. It suggests a real need for poetry as a spoken art. In particular we may take heart from the contemporary use of songs in plays—Sean O'Casey's, for instance, or John Arden's *Sergeant Musgrave's Dance*. Laertes said of his poor, mad sister's singing, "Thought and affliction, passion, hell itself, / She turns to favour and to prettiness". Through lyric, Ophelia's pathos is transmuted into something at once impersonal and in the Yeatsian sense delighting: "Hamlet and Lear were gay, / Gaiety transfiguring all that dread." Let us never forget the way lyric can turn all to favour—its purifying task.

Some poets today are secretly quite happy to write for other poets alone: Mr. Graves makes *no* secret of it; and of course there's a sense in which every poet writes for himself.

But we cannot be pleased with a state of affairs where poetry is nothing but a closed circuit. Communication outside the magic circle is needed: the lyric, which communicates simple matters in a simple way, is a kind of poetry that commends itself to the ear. By engaging themselves in public perform-ance, with or without music— in, let us not be ashamed of it, poetry as a form of entertainment—poets have the best chance of releasing the lyric impulse today.

3. THE STORY LYRIC

In an introduction to the monumental *English and Scottish Popular Ballads*, compiled by Francis James Child, G. L. Kittredge wrote, "A Ballad is a song that tells a story, or—to take the other point of view—a story told in song." It is the subject of the story lyric, as I call it, which will concern us in this chapter. The territory is bounded on one side by the kind of narrative poem—Crabbe's, say, or Scott's *Marmion*, or Tennyson's—in which there is no thought of music, and on the other by such folk-songs as contain no narrative element. There are not a great many of the latter: while it is true that "there is a continuous spectrum in folk-song between the purely lyric and the purely narrative,"[1] few British folk-songs exist which do not reveal the rudiments or the remains of a story. In folk-poetry things happen.

The story lyric has obvious affinities with the pure song-lyric I have already discussed. Both of them tend to deal with a single situation; both are impersonal, avoid moralising for the most part, and use the un-elaborate syntax and vocabulary which make singing easy; and both were in fact sung. We may add to these definitions, so far as the ballad is concerned, that it seems almost entirely unaffected by the fashionable poetic diction of any period, and that the stories it told were believed to be true stories, or else accepted as such with a willing suspension of belief. Beneath the surface, often not far beneath, we find in British ballads, as in those of other countries, a wealth of folklore which is based largely upon pagan superstition; and we shall take note that, in the great era of their composition—from the fifteenth to the end of the seventeenth century—although Britain was a Christian country—the beliefs which dominated her balladry were largely pre-Christian.

The kind of community which produced story lyric was a small, close, homogeneous, rural one, steeped both in superstition and in hero-worship. The themes of the story lyric are sex, violence and the supernatural, as today the basic themes of the tabloid are sex, violence and money. The ballads were a popular form, because they focused the communal spirit. To what extent any given ballad was originally a work of communal creation, we cannot tell for sure: as M. J. C. Hodgart says, "It is now fairly certain that communal improvisation can take place; something like it has been seen in primitive and peasant communities But it is equally certain that it can hardly have produced the ballad versions we possess."

The most distinctive qualities of the ballad are its rapidity and its refusal, like that of the fairytale, either to moralise or to indulge in emotional comment. It is a story pure and simple, stripped down to essentials. Where moral or emotional comment has crept in, an astute editor can be sure he is dealing with a version of a ballad worked over by a relatively late hand. No one who has lived in a peasant community, even today, can have failed to notice the objectiveness of the countryman, the dispassionateness which underlies the glee he takes in gossip—a product of the peasant's innate fatalism. He does not, where a story is concerned, take sides. Karen Blixen noticed it in Africa:

Coloured people do not take sides in a tale, the interest to them lies in the ingeniousness of the plot itself; and the Somali, who in real life have a strong sense of values, and a gift for moral indignation, give these a rest in their fiction.[2]

The ballad is concerned with action, very rarely with the individual emotions of its characters. Here we may find the dourness of the peasant, and his sense that refinements of emotion are luxuries which can be afforded only by his masters. But beneath this, at its source, is the nature of the community, which found in balladry a communal emotion, took no interest in the private feelings of a ballad character, and created plots in which, as Willa Muir has put it, the characters are merely "functions of the action portrayed."

This lack of moralising and emotional digression makes for the rapidity of story lyric. So, of course, does the fact that it was sung. G. H. Gerould[3] has argued that the compression, impersonality, and dramatic nature of ballads, together with their swift action, arose from the practice of singing stories to tunes. But this rapidity of action does not mean rapidity in performance. Willa Muir, who as a girl heard ballad-singers in northeast Scotland (one of the most fruitful sources of ballads in the British Isles), has described the nature of this singing.[4] A ballad was sung undramatically, in "almost a speaking voice": the singer felt no need to put himself over, but could as it were fade into the ballad: the tempo is slow, the vowels long-drawn-out. "The singer's voice is quite impersonal," Mrs. Muir says of Jeannie Robertson:

> She is merely the vehicle through which flows a remarkable sense of duration, almost of inevitable ceremony and ritual. The slow build-up works on one's feelings well beneath the level of consciousness. Behind the words and the tune lie spaces of silence in which one feels the presence of mysteries . . .
> Only gradually did I become aware of the words and the tune she was singing in a clear, high, true impersonal voice. The tone of unhurried assurance would have soothed any infant like a lullaby, despite the tragic starkness of the words.

Mr. Hodgart suggests an analogy between the ballad's method of narration and those of the film and the strip-cartoon. The cartoon uses the momentum of a story to carry the reader over its gaps: it centres upon a hero or heroine whose adventures, though astonishing, come too thick and fast to allow any interstices where he, or the reader, might stop to question their plausibility: like the ballad, the strip-cartoon interjects fragments of dialogue to explain or advance the action; and like the ballad, it creates popular, mythological figures. I once heard an old woman in a Dublin Post office say to another, "Ah, ye're a right mandrake." I was baffled by this, till I discovered a strip-cartoon in an Irish paper, featuring a magician called 'Mandrake'. By its techniques of cutting and montage, the film produces similar effects in a more sophisticated manner. One shot will carry on from the previous, apparently unrelated one, through the impetus of the story, or sometimes through a hidden visual affinity—a cause-and-effect of image, such as we find in poetry.

But, it must be stressed, in ballads as in films it is the objective story which enables the audience to jump the gaps. A modern poem, expressing some private drama of the poet's mind, cannot expect such imaginative leaps unless the reader is highly sophisticated, or unless the poet can clothe this inner drama, as Coleridge did with *The Ancient Mariner*, in a tale which the reader accepts as objective story-telling, and whose deeper meanings come to him through the nature of the external events and the poetic pressure beneath them. The basic difference between *The Ancient Mariner* and a traditional ballad such as *Sir Patrick Spence* is that in the former we are made constantly aware of the Mariner's thoughts and feelings, whereas we get no inkling of Sir Patrick Spence's except when he is reacting to the King's letter.

Mr. Hodgart has used this poem to illustrate the cinematic qualities of ballad, and I cannot do better than enlarge upon his treatment. *Sir Patrick Spence*—the best version of it—

tells the whole story in eleven four-line stanzas. See it as a movie: Shot one, the King sitting in Dumferlinge towne, drinking. He wants a good sailor "to sail this ship of mine": an elderly knight tells him that Sir Patrick is "the best sailor / That sails upon the sea". The King is seen writing a letter. Cut to "Sir Patrick Spence / Was walking on the strand." He reads the first line of the letter and bursts out laughing, reads the next line, and tears come to his eyes— derision and grief that the King, obviously no sailor, should "send me out this time o' the year, / To sail upon the sea." Enter Sir Patrick's shipmaster: dialogue: the man confirms Sir Patrick's fears; he knows the weather signs; late yesterday evening he saw the new moon with the old moon in her arms: a deadly storm is brewing. Cut to a ship sinking—no account of the voyage or the storm: by indirections we are shown what happened:

> O our Scots nobles wer richt laith
> To wet their cork-heild shoone;
> But lang owre a' the play wer playd,
> Their hats they swam aboone.

We have just time to notice the telling visual detail before the scene is whisked away. Cut to the ladies waiting at home with their fans in their hands and gold combs in their hair: a long, long wait, for they will never see their husbands again. Cut to an empty sea, no man and no ship visible—

> Haf owre, haf owre to Aberdour,
> It's fiftie fadom deip,
> And thair lies guid Sir Patrick Spence
> Wi the Scots lords at his feet.

There's this speed and economy in narrative, and this brilliant placing of graphic detail. Like any work of more sophisticated art, the ballad depends as much upon what is left out as what is put in. One thing left out is motive: this version never tells us why or where the King wanted a ship to sail (other versions say it was to fetch the King of Norway's daughter from her country, and they also give us an account of the storm). One could say that the version I have used leaves out the reason for the voyage because the ballad-singers' audience would already be familiar with it. But to my mind it connects with the peasant's lack of curiosity about motive—particularly the motives of his social superiors. Even today the countryman, in my experience, while passionately interested in the doings of such people, very seldom gossips about *why* they do what they do: it was partly this fatalistic, humorous acceptance that, before wars became highly technological, made him such a good soldier: his not to reason why.

The lack of interest in any but the simplest motivation connects, too, with the flatness of character in story lyrics. To particularise a character would make it more difficult for the audience to identify itself with him. The ballad audience, we must remember, was not so much a number of separate individuals as a like-minded group swayed by group emotion —a collection of people welded into one by this emotion, identifying itself with the hero through imagined actions in which their individualities were submerged and a group-response took over. The hero was both a symbol and a conduit: to characterise him would have defeated the ends for which he was created.

When we consider the nature of the ballad, it is difficult to exclude hypotheses about folk memory and the archetypes. Certain stories keep recurring, not only in the British Isles, but in Europe, America, and the East. This is not always just a question of a theme cropping up. Professor Gerould instances the ballad we know as 'Lord Randal' appearing in Czecho-Slovakia, Hungary, Sweden and Calabria, the latter version following in almost exact detail the British one. But of course 'following' is a misleading word: the ballad story, for all we know, may have originated in Calabria and migrated elsewhere. Now it is perfectly true that the trade-routes, especially between Britain, France and Scandinavia, enabled ballads, like folk tales, to move freely about Europe. But some of the key ballad episodes, particularly ones relating to magic—were they disseminated *only* in this way? For instance, the need to keep a grip on a being, through many changes of shape, which emerges from the Proteus story and other Greek legends, crops up again in the British ballad of Tam Lin. Willa Muir suggests that the theme may have originated with the priest-King's substituting animals for his own person as sacrificial victims. Or it may have embodied folk-memory of ordeal and initiation ceremonies: in order to get her lover back, the heroine must keep a grip on him while he is transformed successively into an esk (a newt), an adder, a bear, a lion, a red-hot iron, a burning coal, and then throw him into water.

If we can allow that certain images come to the individual out of a mass unconscious, we have, not necessarily an alternative to conscious oral transmission, but a reason why ballads embodying such images should have been felt to possess special power and therefore been the ones most widely transmitted. But again, it does not follow that the force of a ballad theme must reside in its antiquity. In *The Lore and Language of Schoolchildren*,[5] the Opies have given examples of the way a contemporary theme may catch on, and be disseminated like sparks from a forest fire. "The speed with which a newly made-up rhyme can travel the length and breadth of the country by the schoolchild grapevine," they say, "seems to be little short of miraculous." In 1936, for example, when no mention of the King's possible abdication was allowed in British papers or broadcasting, or even in the music halls, the following rhyme appeared:

> *Hark, the Herald Angels sing,*
> *Mrs. Simpson's pinched our King.*

The rhyme was heard from the lips of children, to the considerable embarrassment of their teachers, in London, in Chichester, in Liverpool, and in Wales. "Little short of miraculous" it certainly is, when we bear in mind that the schoolchildren in question were predominantly working-class and would not be visiting other parts of the country at this time of the year. How was the rhyme carried so fast and so far?

At any rate, we cannot be surprised at the widespread dissemination of story lyrics. At first it was oral; then, with printing, broadside versions began to take over. The carole, a kind of mediaeval story lyric associated with the dance, seems to have preceded the ballad throughout western Europe. The ballad, as we know it, emerged next. 'Judas', the earliest one we can date, comes from the thirteenth century. The sixteenth and seventeenth centuries seem to have been most productive of ballad writing: the period 1749–80, Mr. Hodgart claims, was the one during which many of our great ballads appeared in their most beautiful form. Percy's *Reliques* produced that new interest in folk poetry which we associate with the names of Scott, Burns, and Hogg. But, as I have said, the refining of ballads at this period often led to a certain weakening in their character. The new literary interest in them had another adverse effect: Margaret Laidlaw, Hogg's mother and a noted ballad-singer, complained to Scott that ballads were made for singing and he had "broken the charm" by printing them. Nevertheless, the ballad as a story lyric has survived for two centuries more: about eighty of the Child ballads, for instance, were sung in the United States in 1950; and at the time of writing this, there is a great revival of folk-song on college campuses.

The change-over from oral to written transmission must have been a gradual one. For many years after the broadsides began to be circulated, we may assume that many of the audiences for balladry, and some of the singers, remained illiterate. Since printing would tend to stabilise the form of a ballad, the multiplicity of versions in which most of the ballads are known to us suggests that oral traditions, altering a ballad's words by reason of a singer's faulty memory or his desire to improve upon what he remembers, may have continued side by side with the printed transmission for a good deal longer than is generally allowed. Ballad collectors have testified that folk singers are unaware of the changes they make, yet never sing either words or music exactly like their neighbors, and sometimes sing variants of their own versions. Again, since these makers were in their way professional, we should be unwise to think of such variants as purely accidental: when a singer improvised a new verbal or musical phrase, though not critically conscious of what he was doing, he would be led by an instinct for rightness—an instinct formed by his tradition.

Conversely, we must bear in mind the prestige which print gave to a poem for unsophisticated people. As Mopsa says in *The Winter's Tale*, "I love a ballad in print, a' life: for then we are sure they are true." Karen Blixen tells about the effect upon a native African, Jogona, of a document she gave him setting out the facts of a certain event in which he had been concerned:

> The importance of the account was not lessened but augmented with time, as if to Jogona the greatest wonder about it was that it did not change. The Past, that had been so difficult to bring to memory, and that had probably seemed to be changing every time it was thought of, had here been . . . pinned down before his eyes. It had become History.[6]

We are so inured nowadays to accepting poetry as an art for the minority that it is difficult to put ourselves in the minds of people who knew it as a popular art. It was all very well, the cynic may say, in the sixteenth and early seventeenth century, when the London populace tolerated poetry because Shakespeare and others laced it with a lot of pageantry, clowning and bloodletting, while the countryfolk endured those interminable ballads because in the hideous boredom of the rural winter there was almost nothing else for them to do. Be that as it may, it does not explain how semi-illiterate rustics could produce poems of such remarkable quality, and still less does it help us to determine what that poetic quality is. As with the song lyric, so with the story lyric, our contemporary instruments for analysing and measuring the value of a poem seem to get nowhere.

Let us glance first at this allegedly near-brutish community which produced the story-lyric. Although their ballads do not moralise, certain moral values are implicit in them. The Border ballads, for instance, tell stories which are informed by the qualities most valued in those tough Border communities—faithfulness to one's word, courage and skill in war and love, loyalty to the family or the clan. Move several centuries on and two thousand miles away. Investigating the people in the Southern Highlands of the United States, for whom balladry was an active cultural force, Cecil Sharp noted that they were mostly poor and illiterate, that blood-feuds had been common among them and were still not unknown, that modern communications had not affected them enough to disrupt their traditional way of life, and that they possessed the good manners and proud, easy bearing which had also distinguished the Scots Highland and the Border folk. Again, we get a picture of communities where democratic manners have been shaped by primitive aristocratic tradition—the heroic tradition Yeats sought for, among the Irish peasantry and landowners, of vivid and passionate action, of brimming personality and independence of mind rather than drab nonentity, of courtesy, pride and gaiety.

In his Norton lectures, the late Edwin Muir said of the ballads that they

lie on the other side of the great plateau of the 18th century, with its humanitarian passion and its vast hopes for mankind. And the early tragic world which they summon up was the poetic sustenance of the peasantry for hundreds of years.[7]

Time and again ballad themes blend the tragic view of life, which arises from a peasant fatalism and acceptance, with an heroic quality representing the love of adventure, of bright primary colours, of what Yeats meant by gaiety and Hopkins wrote of as "Honour flashed off exploit". The conclusion of a ballad about love might well be tragic; but the action of the man and woman concerned was passionate, violent and stark in the heroic manner.

The ballad-maker's love of adventure often had to be a vicarious one, unless he was involved in fighting feuds. But in another sense—that of experiencing and recording what is alien—the material of adventure was all around him. Whether his subject was the tragedy of a Queen's lady-in-waiting, Mary Hamilton, or of some humbler person nearer home; whether he made a new song about some local happening, or reproduced a traditional one; he was sustained by the fascination and prestige of action. He lived in a world of what the modern news-editor calls 'human-interest stories' —stories like those of the tabloid, in which murder, incest, suicide, lust, treachery, cruelty, vengeance and jealousy predominate: like Ophelia, he turned it all to favour and to prettiness; and he did so without sentimentalising. His medium, poetry and music, purified the terrible facts of human life by distancing them: the moral squalor of the tabloid never enters into the story lyric: though acts of violence take place, it is noticeable that they are nearly always acts of impulse, done in hot blood; there is little malice prepense, little sordid circumspection.

In a sense, the story lyric is the poor man's epic. We remember Matthew Arnold saying that translations of Homer should be, like their original, "simple, rapid and noble". Simple and rapid the ballad was; and it achieved now and then the nobleness which comes of austerity. Few of us today know the tunes without which this great body of work could not have been created. Yet we can respond to the ballads as poems; and the qualities we respond to are, first and foremost, those of austerity, simpleness, rapidity. It is these qualities which make for the dramatic nature of the ballad —these and, in Professor Gerould's phrase, "the vivid intensity with which the situation is seen." For us, the story *qua* story may not be so important as it was to the ballad audience. What carries us on is the lyricism—the singing line of the words which was made possible by a tune and has survived the tune's vanishing or our ignorance of it.

The most obvious feature of this lyricism is the balladmaker's habit of reiteration and refrain. It is likely that, in its earliest days, the ballad used refrain pretty frequently, and that many refrains disappeared when the function of the audience as a chorus went out, and when ballads began to be printed. But reiteration is a keynote of the ballad throughout its history, as indeed it is of all folk-song.

> *He hadna gane a mile, a mile,*
> *A mile but barely three . . .*

or,

> 'Awa', awa', ye ugly witch,
> Haud far awa', an' let me be!
> I never will be your lemman sae true,
> An' I wish I were out o' your company' . . .

> 'Awa', awa', ye ugly witch,
> Haud far awa', an' let me be!
> For I wouldna once kiss your ugly mouth
> For a' th gifts that ye could gie'.

Such repetitions served several purposes. They provided a mnemonic breathing-space for the singer. They produced an incantatory effect upon the audience, while giving them the pleasure of recognising a phrase or passage already heard. Sometimes it marked a pause between two stages of the action: as Professor Gerould wrote,

> Parallelism of this sort, holding us in suspense for the break that releases the ear while it resolves the situation, cannot fail to tighten the nerves a little.[8]

And I may add to that the changing tempo which repetitions produce in a story. Nothing could be more tedious than a story which is *all* action: the ballad-maker, debarred from pausing to describe the scenery or his characters' emotions in order to vary the narrative tempo, employed the technique of verbal repetition (which of course would be heightened by the tune). I have called the maker a professional; and his professionalism reveals itself not least in the skill and ease with which he employed this rhetorical figure.

There are times when it becomes more than mere incantation or narrative device. It can suggest a deep feeling which might well have moved us less if it had been made explicit. Writing of *Child Waters* that "no more moving tale of self-forgetful love has ever been told," Professor Gerould quotes these stanzas:—

> 'If the child be mine, Faire Ellen,' he sayd,
> 'Be mine, as you tell mee.
> Take you Cheshire and Lancashire both,
> Take them your owne to bee.
>
> 'If the child be mine, Faire Ellen,' he sayd,
> 'Be mine, as you doe sweare,
> Take you Cheshire and Lancashire both,
> And make that child your heyre.'

Shee saies, 'I had rather haue one kisse,
Child Waters, of thy mouth,
Than I wold haue Cheshire and Lancashire both,
That lyes by north and south.

And I had rather haue a twinkling,
Child Waters, of your eye,
Than I wold haue Cheshire and Lancashire both,
To take them mine owne to bee.'[9]

I have spoken of the ballad-maker as one who deals in the alien—the sort of life that indeed may lie all around him, but is not identical with his own or coterminous with it. In his poems he accepts the strangeness of life, as a child does, but at the same time, like a child, is wide open to the sense of wonder. It could be roused, though it rarely was, by such heroic selflessness as fair Ellen showed throughout the ordeals of *Child Waters*: the ballad, accepting this mysterious fact of a woman's loving loyalty, proceeds to heighten it. But the kind of mystery commonest in ballad is that of what we would now call superstition. Animism is constantly cropping up: enchanted trees; talking birds and animals.

It is typical of eighteenth-century rationalism that the bird which convicted Young Hunting's mistress of his murder—and may well have been his own transmigrated soul—should have been called in late versions not just a bird, but a popinjay: parrots *can* talk.

Of the Child ballads, only some twenty-five take the supernatural for their direct subject. But, as L. C. Wimberly has traced in his exhaustive study,[10] our ballad literature is pervaded by folklore, the bulk of which dates back to pagan belief and practice, and whose particulars can sometimes be linked with those of primitive societies in other lands. Christian beliefs are much rarer, and often confused with pagan ones or superimposed upon them. 'The Wife of Usher's Well', for example, hears that her three sons have been lost at sea. Then,

> *It fell about the Martinmas,*
> *When nights are long and mirk*
> *The carline wife's three sons came hame,*
> *And their hats were o' the birk.*

The birch has strong associations with death in pagan mythology: but here it is said to have grown "at the gates o' Paradise". The mother orders a fire to be made, a feast and a bed prepared. We are left in doubt whether or no she deceives herself into thinking her sons are alive: for the ballad-makers, the dead were in any case material revenants, not disembodied spirits, and possibly reflect a period when soul and body were not thought of as separate entities. But presently the youngest son says to the eldest,

> '*The cock doth craw, the day doth daw,*
> *The channerin' worm doth chide;*
> *Gin we be missed out o' our place,*
> *A sair pain we maun bide.*'

In ballads the revenants customarily return to their tombs and lie down. Here a Christian idea of Purgatory has crept in—'a sair pain we maun bide'—and in spite of the birk's growing at the gates of Paradise: at the same time, as Professor Wimberly suggests, "through the crowing of the cock . . . a signal for the departure of the dead to a world of spirits, we may perhaps restore to our tradition a land of gloom comparable to . . . the Norse Niftheim or Hel."

In spite of this confusion between Christian and pagan lore, the ballad makes its effect. Not only the mother, but the sons with their tender compunction about leaving her, behave in a natural way which the supernatural tenor of the story does not render invalid. "The channerin' worm doth chide" is surely one of the hardest-hitting lines in balladry.

And here may I digress for a moment on the subject of worms and the accidents of language? 'Channering' is emotionally disturbing even if we do not know that it means 'fretting'. But the unfortunate young man transformed by Alison Gross into "an ugly worm" and condemned to "toddle about the tree"—our present meaning of 'toddle' makes the picture either quaint or ludicrous, and breaks the spell all too effectively; while the picture of Dives, condemned "To sit upon a serpent's knee," which would not have seemed grotesque to ballad audiences acquainted with mediaeval pictures of hell, to us is merely comic.

We must avoid the form of condescension which would lead us to appreciate ballads for their quaintness. In fact, it is remarkable how seldom this matter of quaintness arises. The supernatural ballads, and indeed many of the others, make their effect as living poetry, not as museum pieces, because they combine clarity of expression with a sense of circumambient mystery. To what extent the maker and his audience, at any given period, 'believed in' the superstitions which pervade the ballads, we cannot tell. All we can be sure of is that such folklore lay deep both in the communal tradition and the individual mind: had it not done so, at least the later versions of the ballads embodying such lore would surely lack conviction—would seem superficial or tainted with antiquarianism. Folklore is imbedded in the ballads, not a decoration imposed upon them. Their makers, no less than the literary poets, were partly concerned to explore the unknown, the alien; and what gives their poetry its depth of emotional meaning was drawn from dark wells to which they had access and which still exist in us though we have bricked them over.

Are we not the more profoundly stirred by the common ballad image of star-crossed lovers changed to intertwining plants, because it derives from an age-old belief that, after death, the soul may pass into a tree? When we read how True Thomas journeyed with the Queen of Elfland—

> O they rade on, and farther on,
> And they waded rivers abune the knee;
> And they saw neither sun nor moon,
> But they heard the roaring of the sea.
>
> It was mirk, mirk night, there was nae starlight,
> They waded thro' red blude to the knee;
> For a' the blude that's shed on the earth
> Rins through the springs o' that countrie.

—layers of ancestral memory stir in us. The ancient belief that one must go through water or blood to the Otherworld; the river Styx; Odysseus' blood-offering to his dead comrades: the belief that fairies lived inside the earth, where sun and moon and stars were invisible. When he first met the Queen of Elfland, Thomas hailed her as "Mary, Queen of Heaven": there are Christian references, too, in the paths of Righteousness and Wickedness which the Queen shows him. Chiefly, the ballad reveals that confusion between fairies and the dead, the underworld and the fairy world, so common in folklore: in Scandinavia, 'elves' was once a name for the dead. But my point is that to produce the finest, most resonant stanzas in the poem, its maker drew upon the deepest sources of folk memory: is it not our own more deeply buried but not extinct folk-memory which causes us to respond to them as we do?

Would Keats have been able to make so haunting a poem of 'La Belle Dame Sans Merci' had he merely taken the surface story of 'Thomas the Rhymer', and not broken through to the deeper levels from which it was composed? We may be fairly sure that 'La Belle Dame' is a subjective poem, imaging the poet's own experience of love and thraldom, whereas 'Thomas the Rhymer' is not. But otherwise the two poems have much in common, much that derives from folklore. Both men meet a fairy and go off with her on a horse. Both accept food from her—an extremely dangerous thing to do whether it's honey and manna dew or an apple (compare the legend of Eve, and Persephone's tasting of pomegranate seeds in the Underworld). Both men kiss her, which is quite fatal, for a kiss puts you in a fairy's power (a kiss can also, in folklore, be a way of breaking a thrall—Beauty and the Beast). The topography of the poems is vague: but fairies live inside hills, and Keats' Belle Dame has an elfin *grot*, and later his knight dreams and awakes on the cold *hill's side*. His dream of pale kings and warriors, ensorcelled by love, carries surely an echo of the belief that fairies spirited human beings away to pay their tribute to hell. I am not speculating about the extent either of Keats' folklore knowledge or of his debt to the anonymous ballad-maker (the only reference to the poem in his letters is a facetious one): all I suggest is that, by accident or design, Keats tapped in this poem a vein of great psychic potency, and that in responding to it we get an inkling of the way a ballad audience was thrilled.

'La Belle Dame Sans Merci' catches one characteristic of the traditional ballad supremely well, as Professor Gerould points out—the maker's power, while often barely hinting at the story, to leave us in no doubt what happened. But we cannot pretend that if, never having seen the Keats poem before, we had found it in a book of anonymous ballads, we should mistake it for one. 'La Belle Dame' is softer in tone, smoother in technique, more romantic and personal than any poem of the balladry of tradition: nor, incidentally, could we imagine it sung in the folk-tune manner. That such a tradition existed (and indeed still does in re-creations by modern folk-singers) is surely undeniable. Professor Gerould writes,

> . . . we are forced to accept belief in a tradition of artistry current at least in certain groups or families and in certain regions, and probably continuing from century to century, which has guided the re-making of folk-songs. Without the existence of such a tradition, the changes inevitable when words and music are transmitted orally would have resulted in the swift destruction of any beauty, and *a fortiori* could not have produced the parallel versions of considerable merit . . .[11]

When the literary poet ventures upon the story lyric, he may, as Coleridge did, produce a work of greater scope and significance than any of the anonymous ballads; but in doing so he will break away from many of the staples that constitute ballad tradition. The most evident of these is music and the presence of a listening group. Few poems by such writers combine successfully the narrative and the folk-music elements, as Scott contrived to do in 'Proud Maisie': his 'Marmion' has a ballad movement, so do Macaulay's 'Lays of Ancient Rome'; but these poems are not for singing, and they differ from the traditional ballad in telling the story extensively, with few of the links omitted. What the literary poets give us for the most part is narrative with a lyrical flavour, and this parallels the change from song lyric to lyrical poetry which I discussed earlier. The story lyric, throughout the late eighteenth and nineteenth centuries, shows that increase of romanticism about love, and of self-consciousness, which Mrs. Muir notices even in late ballads or ballad versions of the traditional type: 'Helen of Kirkconnell', for instance, 'is a very beautiful poem, but it points and dwells upon the hero's emotions as earlier ballads do not.'

What the older makers gave us was action as ritual. After the great age of balladry, the story lyric becomes at the hands

of literary poets more realistic and more subjective: on the
one side we get Browning's dramatic lyrics, on the other
Crabbe's 'Sir Eustace Grey'. A third development should also
be noted: Sidney Dobell's remarkable poem, 'The Orphan's
Song', uses reiteration freely, plays down the story element
and brings up the lyrical, so as to give us a sort of literary
equivalent of folksong. Or again, the story element is sub-
dued to the singing one in 'The Trees So High', a late but
attractive version of the old ballad, 'Still Growing'. Here are
the first three stanzas of it:

> *All the trees they are so high*
> *The leaves they are so green,*
> *The day is past and gone, sweet-heart,*
> *That you and I have seen,*
> *It is cold winter's night,*
> *You and I must bide alone;*
> *Whilst my pretty lad is young*
> *And is growing.*
>
> *In a garden as I walked,*
> *I heard them laugh and call;*
> *There were four and twenty playing there,*
> *They played with bat and ball.*
> *O the rain on the roof,*
> *Here and I must make my moan;*
> *.Whilst my pretty lad is young*
> *And is growing.*
>
> *I listened in the garden,*
> *I look'd o'er the wall;*
> *'Midst five and twenty gallants there*
> *My love exceeded all.*
> *O the wind on the thatch,*
> *Here and I alone must weep;*
> *Whilst my pretty lad is young*
> *And is growing.*

Of this poem, as of many others by known or anonymous writers who worked in the ballad form after the Enlightenment, one may say that something feminine has crept in—a sensibility we do not find in earlier ballad versions.

This sensibility is an awkward thing to accommodate within a form perfected by people who lacked it. The softness and insipidity of so many Victorian ballad-poems witness to the decadence which sets in when sensitive poets aim at a simplicity and toughness not in their nature. Kipling could use ballad form effectively because, though a vulnerable man, he was not a noticeably sensitive one, and because he chose virile subjects. Yeats was a highly sensitive man; but his love of the heroic and his contempt for passive suffering as a theme for poetry enabled him to write truly modern poems—'The Rose Tree', for example—which are like grafts from the purest ballad stock. Thomas Hardy in 'A Trampwoman's Tragedy', wrote a poem whose use of refrain, lyrical movement, and powerful story are close to the ballad tradition; but idiosyncrasies of language and a certain leisureliness in the telling set it apart.

At a further remove lie the story lyrics of our own time which present dramatic episodes in lyrical language, but retain little or no vestige of ballad techniques. We could point to Browning's 'Meeting at Night' as a forerunner of these: some of Hardy's 1912–13 poems, written after his first wife's death, are story lyrics of the utmost poignancy. Robert Graves' 'The Foreboding', which tells a personal dramatic event in language at once lyrical and conventionally flexible, is a model of the way this medium should be handled:—

> *Looking by chance in at the open window*
> *I saw my own self seated in his chair*
> *With gaze abstracted, furrowed forehead*
> *Unkempt hair.*

I thought that I had suddenly come to die,
*   That to a cold corpse this was my farewell,*
Until the pen moved slowly on the paper
*   And tears fell.*

He had written a name, yours, in printed letters—
*   One word on which bemusedly to pore:*
No protest, no desire, your naked name,
*   Nothing more.*

Would it be tomorrow, would it be next year?
*   But the vision was not false, this much I knew;*
And I turned angrily from the open window
*   Aghast at you.*

Why never a warning, either by speech or look,
*   That the love you cruelly gave me could not last?*
Already it was too late; the bait swallowed,
*   The hook fast.*[12]

Such poems are unaccompanied by even the ghost of a tune. But certain British poets of today—W. H. Auden, for instance, William Plomer, and Charles Causley—fascinated by ballad form, have sought to use it fairly strictly, to tell a modern story or express a modern state of mind. All three poets, each in his own way, have produced poems which are genuine developments of ballad, not clever pastiches; moreover, Auden wrote some of his to be sung in cabaret.

As I walked out one evening,
*   Walking down Bristol Street,*
The crowds upon the pavement
*   Were fields of harvest wheat.*

And down by the brimming river
*   I heard a lover sing*
Under an arch of the railway:
*   'Love has no ending . . .'*

So the poem begins, a straightforward folk-song apparently. It develops, with an absolute minimum of story, into a dialogue between the lover and Time, the latter speaking in the young Auden's most minatory manner:—

> 'The glacier knocks on the cupboard,
>   The desert sighs in the bed,
> And the crack in the tea-cup opens
>   A lane to the land of the dead.'[13]

We know where we are now, and it is a very long distance from 'the channerin' worm doth chide'. Metaphor, so rare in traditional ballad, plays a major part: in almost any ballad by a modern, sophisticated poet we shall find the presence of under-meanings, the story employing action in such a way as to suggest social or psychological commentary.

This seems to me inevitable. And another feature of modern ballad is that it tends to load the dice. The impersonality of the traditional ballad, its refusal to take sides, has been replaced by a satirical or moralising tone, at times by a cruelty quite different from the dispassionate treatment of violence which the anonymous makers afford us. There is something merciless about William Plomer's ballads, such as 'Slightly Foxed', or 'The Widow's Plot', or 'Mews Flat Mona', or 'The Self-Made Blonde', as there is in Auden's 'Miss Gee' and even in 'Victor'. This, again, is inevitable; for the modern sensibility, shrinking from the violent or sordid events which the traditional ballad took in its stride, yet at the same time covertly fascinated by them, is impelled to examine the springs of violence in itself, and in doing so may become infected by them: it is the need to cauterise the infected part, I suggest, that produces this rather heartless, brutal, satirical tone we notice in many modern ballads. The traditional balladist is hard in a quite unselfconscious way; the modern one, because he is afraid to be soft.

Here, then, is one way in which the literary poet modifies
the ballad for his own purposes. Another is through a sophistication less of attitude than of language: we find it in Louis
MacNeice's 'The Streets of Laredo', a poem sung to the
original American cowboy tune, on the subject of the London
blitzes. It begins.

> O early one morning I walked out like Agag,
> Early one morning to walk through the fire
> Dodging the pythons that leaked on the pavements
> With tinkle of glasses and tangle of wire;[14]

We get it in the ballads of Charles Causley, which have a
flighty, erratic movement, great gaiety of language, and at
times an almost surrealist play of metaphor—

> While the children danced all over the hill
>   I cut the corn with Looney Lil
> She didn't know what was three times seven
>   But she unscrewed her eyes and showed me heaven
> I pillowed my head on her wounded breast
>   And the sun baled out in the bleeding west.[15]

The danger for the contemporary balladist is that, in
straining hard to avoid pastiche and anachronism, he may
produce a too obviously self-conscious poem which will affect
us like an artificial flower masquerading as a real rose. There
is also the danger of putting in more 'psychology' or a greater
weight of metaphor than the form will bear; since, though
it cannot be simple in the way of its predecessors, the modern
ballad still needs to be rapid. Here, it evidently helps the
poet if he has a folk-tune in his head, for such a tune will
set the pace. Risks have to be taken; and it is an encouraging
matter that, as well as the story lyric which has broken away
from ballad form, we have this form still very much alive,
not only in contemporary folk-singing, but in the experi-

ments of literary poets. Magic, in the folklore sense, may no longer be available; but mystery there is, and the magical effect words have upon us when a poet, delivering them from dead routine, releases them into the figures of a new and living dance.

4. THE COMMON MUSE

tin-horn verse

In Book Five of *The Prelude,* paying his tribute to "all books which lay / Their sure foundations in the heart of man", Wordsworth celebrates not only Greek and Jewish literature, but

> *Those trumpet-tones of harmony that shake*
> *Our shores in England—from those loftiest notes*
> *Down to the low and wren-like warblings, made*
> *For cottagers and spinners at the wheel,*
> *And sun-burnt travellers resting their tired limbs,*
> *Stretched under wayside hedge-rows, ballad tunes,*
> *Food for the hungry ears of little ones,*
> *And of old men who have survived their joys . . .*

Wordsworth, in fact, seems to have been more interested by the street ballad than by the traditional story-lyric with which the preceding chapter was concerned: and whatever one may say about the tunes of the former, "low and wren-like warblings" can hardly apply to their words, which tend to be rude and raucous. As Douglas Jerrold said about the street ballad-singer, "If he were not the clear silver trump of Fame, he was at least her tin horn." It is this tin-horn verse that I shall look at now, primarily as we meet it in the street ballad; but I want also to discuss the broader results of urban life and the industrial revolution upon lyrical poetry.

The first thing that must strike us when we compare the traditional ballad with the street ballad is that, although for some time they ran concurrently, and although they both represented a popular poetry, they should be such worlds apart in tone and quality. V. de S. Pinto and A. E. Rodway, introducing their excellent anthology whose title I have borrowed for this chapter, set out the differences between the two types of popular verse; I can do no better than summarise the points they make. First,

> If there is one typical quality common to all street ballads, with only a very few exceptions, it is that they are "low-faluting" . . . Thus the street ballads, though sometimes ingeniously fantastic rather than realistic, are nevertheless typically unsentimental, uncourtly and irreverent when they deal with the subject of love.[1]

The street ballad originated in a less simple world than the traditional. An urban product, it was not informed by folklore and superstition. It "tended to be comic, realistic and unheroic", as the traditional ballad "tended to be tragic, romantic and heroic". Its diction is less standardised: it is much more topical in its subjects, much more in the nature of occasional verse. It seldom uses the cinematic technique of "vivid dreamlike images", and tells its story less rapidly. I would add to these distinctions that the street ballad indulges in moralising and commentary to an extent we never find even in the latest versions of the traditional story-lyric; and *pace* Pinto and Rodway, its poetic quality—if we except ballads written by good professional poets—is vastly inferior.

What W. Henderson writes about Victorian street ballads is true for the most part of their predecessors:

> Many of them are mere doggerel; but it is no paradox to say that their illiteracy is a positive merit. Their writers, themselves unlettered, belonged to a class that was all but inarticulate. In these rough ballads . . . the poor and wretched found a voice— a voice harsh and untuneful, indeed, yet endued with a certain fitness of its own.[2]

In fact, the interest of the street ballad is a mainly sociological one. And not only to us: one of Queen Elizabeth's

Ministers used to scan the broadsides of his time, seeing how they took on with the people, and making his dispositions accordingly. He was doing what the astute politician does today—keeping his finger on the pulse of the nation by reading the popular press.

It is here, in the social attitude and criticism expressed or implied, that the street ballad diverges most widely from the traditional. But this is only one aspect of the difference between the popular verse thrown up by an urban and by a rural community, the one sceptical, radical, topical, the other accepting, conservative, and distanced. Country people were willing to hear an old story told and retold for centuries: townsfolk more and more wanted the very latest one, hot from the press (the modern journalist still calls his copy 'a story'). One reason for the street ballad's inferiority is that its writer often had less time to imagine himself into the situation he wrote about than had the traditional balladist. It seems probable that street-ballads existed before the introduction of printing: the robust "London Lickpenny", which gives a lively picture of a Kentish countryman discovering the law's delays and the city streets, dates from the second half of the fifteenth century. But it was the broadside, growing from a trickle to a flood towards the end of Elizabeth's reign, which established the popularity of the medium. In 1600 the essayist, William Cornwallis, watches a ballad-singer and his audience, and draws a rather toffee-nosed moral from his observations:—

The profit, to see earthlings satisfied with such coarse stuff, to leave vice rebuked, and to see the power of vertue that pierceth the head of such a base historian and vile auditorie. The recreation, to see how thoroughly the standers by are affected, what strange gestures come from them, what strayned stuff from their poet, what shift they make to stand to heare, what extremities he is driven to for rime . . .

Cornwallis might well have been listening to the ballad, made about sixteen years before, on the Queen's reception of Sir Francis Drake after his voyage round the world, two stanzas of which show all too clearly what "strayned stuff" and desperate gropings for rhyme the singer was driven to:

> Then came the Lord Chamberlain with his white staff,
> And all the people began to laugh;
> And then the Queen began to speak,
> 'You're welcome home, Sir Francis Drake.'
>
> You gallants all o' the British blood,
> Why don't you sail o' the ocean flood?
> I protest you're not all worth a filbert
> If once compared to Sir Humphrey Gilbert.

The subjects of street balladry were very much those of the modern popular newspaper. Sex-encounters, battles, catastrophes, fires, floods, freaks and monsters; fashions and foibles; murder, conspiracy, execution: political subjects had to be treated with a wary eye upon the party in power, as did religious ones. Some of the best early ballads are those of social protest—"The Map of Mock-Beggar Hall", for instance, or "The Poor Man Pays for All", or "The Old Courtier and the New", with its Yeatsian refrain—"Like an old Courtier of the Queen's,/And the Queen's old Courtier". Every aspect of love, except the romantic one, was treated—sometimes with great scurrility; even Nashe, by no means a strait-laced man, was shocked by some of the ballads he heard: the tone of many of these, like that of the social-criticism ballads, is sardonic or ribald, for the poor man relished, as he has always done, other people's predicaments —particularly those of his social superiors—whether on the scaffold or in the bed.

Class distinctions, on the other hand, had not through the sixteenth century ossified into barriers between one kind of entertainment and another. Rich or poor, anyone in Shakespeare's audience would be able to pick up the playwright's allusions to ballad lines and tunes. Equally, Greek and Roman legends, no less than Bible stories, appealed to this heterogeneous audience. One of the oldest ballads of the period, written long before Shakespeare's play, is about Troilus: Aeneas, Penelope, Midas, Diana and Actaeon, Atalanta are other subjects of street balladry. When English became the language of most poets of Ireland, there was a similar recourse to classical myth, encouraged first, it may be, by hedge-schoolmasters, then picked up and garbled by ballad-singers as this stanza of a song about Lovely Katie of Liskehaun.

If Jason famous had known young Katie,
With her he'd sail to the Persian shore,
And hold Ulysses for to release her,
The briney regions he would search o'er.
And you know Paris the Trojan hero,
Who brought Queen Helen to King Priam.
He would venture greater his bride to make her—
Sweet lovely Katie of Liskehaun.[3]

In England, towards the end of the sixteenth century, the street ballad seems to have moved away from classical, biblical and historical subjects to more topical ones. The famous story of the Babes in the Wood, for example, which appeared in 1595, recounted a recent happening—how a Norfolk gentleman, dying, committed his children to the care of his wicked brother. The stress laid upon domestic tragedy at this time set up an ambivalent attitude towards balladry: on the one hand, a condemned criminal might glory in the idea that his crime and execution would become the subject of a rhyme —exhibitionism is common enough among delinquents to-day: on the other hand, Shakespeare makes Cleopatra dread lest, if she goes to Rome, "saucy lictors/Will catch at us like strumpets; and scald rhymers/Ballad us out o' tune": while a criminal in Massinger's *Bondman* begs not to be executed twice—

> *At the gallows first, and after in a ballad*
> *Sung to some hideous tune. There are ten-groat rhymers*
> *About the town, grown fat on these occasions.*
> *Let but a chapel fall, or street be fired,*
> *A foolish lover hang himself for pure love,*
> *Or any such like accident, and before*
> *They are cold in their graves some damned ditty's made*
> *Which makes their ghosts walk.*

In the broadsides, then, topical subjects began to super-sede traditional stories. For three centuries thereafter, until the rise of a cheap popular press, they performed its function of putting out 'sensational' news, human-interest stories, and questions of the day. The broadsides originated in city life, but were disseminated, as Autolycus shows us, through coun-try districts too. They appealed to simple folks' love of a story; and their continued vigour lay partly in this and partly because they represented, so to speak, a *communal* news-paper. If we think of the modern commuter, crouched jeal-ously over his paper like a dog over a bone, isolated in a packed railway compartment, and set him beside the ballad-singer's audience who participated with the singer and with

one another in the little dramas he retailed, we can understand the street-ballad's enduring influence. The singer spoke
the same language as his listeners: he was one of them, and
at one with them.

What was this language? Commonly, it lacks art: robust
it may be; but there is something amateurish about the street
ballads which, quite as much as the nature of their subject
matter, prevents them from being memorable. Unlike most
of the traditional ballads, they have little life when divorced
from the tunes they were sung to. No doubt some of them
were written by educated men who had come down in the
world and wished to turn an honest penny; but these would
have to adapt themselves to the medium in which they
worked—a way of saying things that was acceptable to a
relatively unlettered audience. This amateurishness is most
evident in the street-ballad's lack of finish. By 'finish', I do
not mean a smoothness or consistency in the texture of the
verse, though here these ballads are often inadequate enough:
what is most noticeable to me is the writer's failure to sustain
the 'attack' of his poem, and particularly to end it firmly: so
many broadside poems peter out rather than finish.

"The Death of Admiral Benbow', for instance, starts off
with a rousing lyric movement—

> Come all you sailors bold
> Lend an ear, lend an ear;
> Come all you sailors bold, lend an ear:
> 'Tis of our admiral's fame,
> Brave Benbow call'd by name;
> How he fought on the main
> You shall hear, you shall hear.

But in the version given by Pinto and Rodway, after Benbow's captains have turned tail and a chain-shot has removed
his legs, the final stanza is indeterminate and an anticlimax.

A similar lack of confidence is shown in the many street ballads which conclude with a thumping but perfunctory moral (Swift mimicked this in his satirical ballad on the Archbishop of Dublin—"Then God preserve his Lordship's Grace, and make him live as long / As did Methusalem of old, and so I end my song") One must allow, though, that the balladist could conceal a feeble or a superficial ending by the *rallentando* and *crescendo* he gave to his tune.

The leisurely nature of the street-ballad, the need to spin out a story, not concentrating like the traditional ballad upon a single dramatic episode, was one reason for thinness and unevenness. Another was simply a lack of skill in handling the considerable variety of metre and stanza-form which the street balladists attempted. The basic 4–4 or 4–3 stress of the traditional ballad, sanctified by long usage, was in the singer's blood and easy to manage compared with these more elaborate measures: it is worth remarking that perhaps the finest of all broadside poems, 'Hierusalem, my happie home', was written in the simple 4–3 metre; also, it was almost certainly written by a priest, who had other things to do than aiming at a popular success.

An immediate awareness of one's audience, and particularly of the need to win them, has for three centuries been less and less conducive to good poetry. Nevertheless, it may seem surprising that the street balladist should have relied so little, until Victorian times, on that strain of sentiment which is one way of pleasing an audience. Was he still under the influence of the traditional ballad, in its apparent lack of heart? Was it that the urban poor could afford sensibility no more than good clothes and food?—even today, in a prosperous English working-class home, sons will tease their old Mum quite mercilessly, as though they were ashamed or unable to express their real affection. However this may be, it is rarely that one finds in a street ballad the lyric tone which comes of simple feeling. Here it is, in the last three stanzas

of a ballad in which a girl laments for her lover, a coal-miner
who has been recruited into the army:—

> *As I walked over the stubble field,*
>   *Below it runs the seam,*
> *I thought o' Jimmy Lewin there,*
>   *But it was all a dream.*
>
> *He hewed the very coals we burn,*
>   *And when the fire I'se leetin,*
> *To think the lumps was in his hands,*
>   *It sets my heart to beatin.*
>
> *So break my heart, and then it's ower,*
>   *So break my heart, my dearie,*
> *And I'll lie in the cold, cold grave,*
>   *For of single life I'm weary.*

This poem, so touching and sincere, free from the artificial
floweriness which broadside writers sometimes used in an
attempt to ape the literary poets, is taken from a fine collection by A. L. Lloyd, *Come All Ye Bold Miners.*[4] The Collection includes other good ballads and songs—'The Plodder
Seam', for instance. The success of these coalfield ballads
does suggest that a small, close, homogeneous community
like that of the miners, with jealously preserved traditions of
its own, was more fruitful ground for the ballad than the
relatively heterogeneous and loosely knit populace of a large
town: a parallel might be found in the railroad and cowboy
songs of the United States. The British sailor's community
produced work shanties but few ballads, perhaps because,
though tight and traditional as the miner's, it was less stable,
a ship's company being paid off and dispersed after the
voyage.

To return for a moment to the question of feeling. The
street ballad rarely expressed the feelings of passion or affection, and when it did so the result was apt to be awkward or

conventional. Compare the stanzas just quoted from 'The Recruited Collier' with this one from a ballad on the same theme, 'The Wandering Maiden':

> Over hills and high mountains
>   long time have I gone,
> Ah! and down by the fountains,
>   by myself all alone:
> Through bushes and briers
>   being void of all care,
> Through perils and dangers,
>   for the loss of my dear.

The ballad is simple all right, but it is conventionally poetic: we are not made to care about this maiden's loss, as we do about the suffering of the collier's girl. Simplicity is not enough. There has to be that full acceptance of emotion and then the conscious purifying of it, which we find in the love lyrics of Burns; or else a happy accident such as we occasionally meet in children's poems—a phrase fortuitous and felicitous, transcending the writer's normal power of expression.

Let me give you a ballad where the feeling of deep affection, restrained in our tight-lipped, grudging, North-country way, bursts out at the last line and finds a harsh, perfect word—'scraped'—to utter the speaker's violence of emotion. 'Micky Thumps', although it was in fact a recitation-piece at Lancashire smoking-concerts, has the movement and refrain of a sung street ballad.

> As I was going down Treak Street
> For half a pound of treacle,
> Who should I meet but my old friend Micky Thumps.
> He said to me, 'Will thou come to our wake?'
> I thought a bit,
> I thought a bit,
> I said I didn't mind:
> So I went.

As I was sitting on our doorstep
Who should come by but my old friend
      Micky Thumps' brother.
He said to me, 'Wilt thou come to our house?
Micky is ill.'
I thought a bit,
I thought a bit,
I said I didn't mind:
So I went.

And he were ill:
He were gradely ill.
He said to me,
'Wilt thou come to my funeral, mon, if I die?'
I thought a bit,
I thought a bit,
I said I didn't mind:
So I went.

And it were a funeral.
Some stamped on his grave:
Some spat on his grave:
But I scraped my eyes out for my old friend
      Micky Thumps.

What is lacking for the most part in the numerous street ballads concerned with love is the touch of tenderness. Love is treated in earthy, ungentle terms. The man tries to get his girl without marriage; she adopts the time-honoured methods of defeating his tactics; or else she yields, for the girls are as lusty as the men and welcome the discoveries of the body. If a girl is seduced and deserted, she may go to London to take up the game professionally. Country girls—at any rate in the broadsides written primarily for rural consumption— are held up as superior to town girls, healthier, less affected, less mercenary. Fornication and adultery are a great romp, treated in a rollicking way, sometimes with a wealth of ponderous innuendo and double-entendre. Like the mother-in-law more recently, sex is a stock joke, and the variations upon it are few. It is all a mixture of heartiness about the facts of life with indifference towards its feelings: fine feelings, even if the balladist had them at his command, would have cut little ice with his street-corner audience.

There are exceptions, of course—poems in which the prevailing, reductive idiom of the street love-ballad gives way to a more poetic lyric note. The well-known 'Phillida flouts me' is one of these; another, the early 'Come Turn to me, Thou pretty little one': or there's 'The Happy Husbandman', which celebrates charmingly the delights of country lovers—

> *My young Mary do's mind the dairy*
> *While I go a Howing and Mowing each Morn:*
> *Then hey the little Spinning-Wheel*
> *Merrily round do's reel,*
>   *while I am singing amidst the corn:*
> *Cream and kisses are both my delight,*
> *She gives me them, and the joys of night;*
> *She's soft as the Air, as Morning fair,*
> *Is not such a maid a most pleasing sight? . . .*[5]

Stanzas such as this have a freshness, an authentic feel of the country, quite different from the more polished but less down-to-earth pastorals of literary poets. In general, however, English street ballads on rural themes seem to lack the resonance and ease of country folk-song—of 'Waly, waly', for example, or 'The Sweet Banks of the Primroses', or 'Water-Cresses'.

Irish street balladry of the eighteenth and nineteenth centuries seems in general nearer akin to indigenous folk-song than was the English. Some ballads were written in Irish, phonetically printed; others were bilingual: many were sung to airs different from those of the professional ballad-singer. Like the English street-ballad, the Irish told little stories in a rangy, discursive way, but its treatment of love themes tended to be more lyrical and romantic, less ribald and earthy. Themes of exile are naturally more common; and there is a wealth of patriotic ballads, from 'The Boys of Wexford' to 'The Croppy Boy', reminding us that for five centuries Ireland was an occupied country, which never forgot its struggle against England, its patriots and martyrs— Edward Fitzgerald, Wolfe Tone, Robert Emmet, O'Connell, Parnell, Kevin Barry, and the rest.

The vein of comic hyperbole, so frequent in traditional Irish folk-story and verse, emerges in such street ballads as 'Johnny, I hardly knew ye'; while the native vivacity of that poem is seldom far below the surface—you can hear it, for instance, in 'The Sporting Races of Galway', a ballad which has the same kind of spiritedness, though none of the satire, that we get in Louis MacNeice's 'Bagpipe Music':

. . . It's there you'll see confectioners with sugarsticks and dainties,
The lozenges and oranges, the lemonade and raisins.
The gingerbread and spices to accommodate the ladies,
And a big crubeen for threepence to be picking while you're able.

It's there you'll see the gamblers, the thimbles and the garters,
And the sporting Wheel of Fortune with the four and twenty
    quarters.
There was others without scruple pelting wattles at poor Maggy,
And her father well contented and he looking at his daughter . . .[6]

I cannot resist putting in here a fragment of a Dublin street ballad about the finding of Moses:

In Agypt's land, contaygious to the Nile,
Old Pharo's daughter went to bathe in style.
She tuk her dip and came unto the land,
And for to dry her royal pelt she ran along the strand.
A bull-rush tripped her, whereupon she saw
A smiling babby in a wad of straw.
She took it up and said in accents mild,
'Tare-an-ages, girls, which o' yees owns the child?'[7]

Finally, it is worth mentioning one great Irish tune, which links the street ballad with the highly wrought texture of traditional verse in the Irish language, and with certain poems by English writers. P. J. McCall made his 'On Boolavogue as the sun was setting' from this tune: 'Youghal Harbour' was written to it: 'Sweet County Wexford', another street-ballad, employed a variation of the tune. In 'The bells of Shandon that sound so grand on/The pleasant waters of the river Lee', Father Prout over-exploited the opportunity for assonance presented by the tune's rhythm. Thomas Hardy used it in 'I need not go', and W. H. Auden for a section of his 'Hymn to Saint Cecilia'. I myself employed it for Damon's song in Virgil's Eighth Eclogue. Below is the first stanza of 'Youghal Harbour', in which the assonance of 'alarmed', 'charmer' and 'harbour' is noticeable in the last two lines.

As I roved out on a summer's morning
Early as the day did dawn,
When Sol appeared in pomp and glory
I took my way through a pleasant lawn.
Where pinks and violets were sweetly blooming
And linnets warbling in ev'ry shade.
I've been alarmed by a killing charmer,
Near Youghal Harbour I met this maid.[8]

We must think of the Common Muse, then, as a popular entertainer first and foremost. She wished only to please the customers: she could best please them by singing about things that immediately interested them, to tunes they knew or could quickly master. Town-bred herself, she catered for the crowd rather than for a community—a crowd which was more mobile, excitable, shallow and sceptical than the audience of the traditional ballad-singer. The townsman's clamour for the new meant that, although there are differing broadside versions of some of the street ballads, there is not the long process of refinement which traditional ballads all went through: the Common Muse had a far greater variety of subject matter, but a far lesser opportunity for that imaginative concentration which produces art. Her audience was constantly swelled by countryfolk migrating to the city, men and women who had pulled up their old roots but could not put down flourishing new ones through the mud and cobblestones of the street. An unlettered, primitive audience is always ripe for poetry: people whose way of life leads them to substitute knowingness for wisdom, novelty for tradition, a veneer of sophistication for a core of simplicity—such people are forming that concourse of the half-baked to which poetry can appeal only at its lowest levels.

"In the Elizabethan period," Pinto and Rodway tell us in *The Common Muse*, "there had been a sharp distinction between the balladmonger and the courtly and educated poets. In the seventeenth century, however, scholars and courtiers began to take an interest in popular poetry." Collections of broadsides were made by Selden, Pepys and Sackville: Restoration poets "often write in the manner of the street ballads." This is beyond question; but two points are worth making here. First, just as the street balladist sometimes aped the manners of literary poets, producing florid and artificial phrases, so the literary poet, particularly when he was using the street-ballad manner for propaganda purposes, sometimes roughened his style deliberately so as to attract a popular audience. If this is to employ the Common Muse as a common prostitute, I can hardly censure it, for some of us were doing rather the same thing in our political verse of the Thirties. Let me take one example of this roughening:—

> *The Londoners Gent to the King do present*
> *   In a Box the City Maggot;*
> *'Tis a thing full of weight, that requires the Might*
> *   Of whole Guild-Hall Team to drag it.*
>
> *Whilst their Church's unbuilt, and their Houses undwelt,*
> *   And their Orphans want Bread to feed 'em;*
> *Themselves they've bereft of the little Wealth they had left,*
> *   To make an offering of their Freedom.*

Those are the first two stanzas of a poem by Andrew Marvell satirising the presentation of their Freedoms by London's Lord Mayor and Aldermen to the late King and the Duke of York, in 1674.

But, when literary poets borrowed the street-ballad manner, as did on occasion Suckling, Dorset, Sedley, Rochester, Congreve, Carey, Swift, Prior and Gay, the poems that resulted are generally superior to the products of street balladry plain and simple. They are superior because they have a point and edge, a balance and neatness and resource, to which the humbler versifier rarely attained. This is to say no more than that the talented poet, even when adopting a popular idiom or writing pastiche of it, will bring to it a grace of his own: and this would not need to be said but for the implication made by some over-zealous partisans of the Common Muse that polish, intelligence, grace, are to be equated with weakness, preciosity, or decadence. Chekhov, in a letter to Gorki, defined the operative word: "When a person expends the least possible movement on a certain act, that is grace"—a judgment as true for writing as it is for athletic pursuits. We do no service to the Common Muse by claiming uncommon virtues for her. It was not she, but John Dryden, who brought the 'poetry of statement' to its highest pitch: nevertheless, but for her groundwork in the singing of controversial matters, would *Absalom and Achitopel* have been written?

The Common Muse was a town-bred girl: from this her merits and defects can be seen to spring. Because they were written for singing, the broadside ballads retain something of the lyric impulse, however rude, however diluted. Apart from them, urban poetry in England has seldom tapped the lyrical vein, and never kept it open for long. I do not mean, of course, that lyric poets cannot live in cities: I mean that, despite the devoted efforts of many, they have not yet succeeded in creating a strain of lyricism in which the sights and sounds common to city-dwellers produce their own specific music, or the detail of urban life can move naturally into metaphor and be at home there. Almost all the best town poetry, up to our own century at any rate, has been descriptive, comic, moralising or dramatic, not lyrical: no lyric poetry, but for William Blake's, gives me that sense of deep intimacy with town life which I get from Massinger, say, or Pope, from Johnson's *London* or Gay's *Trivia*, or Browning's *How it Strikes a Contemporary*. Not till the early work of T. S. Eliot can I detect a note of lyricism which sounds native, as it were, to urban civilisation; in making this breakthrough, Eliot was influenced, we know, by Laforgue, and more indirectly by Baudelaire and Rimbaud.

Lyric, in the sense of words-with-music, being the oldest form of poetry, has its roots deep in pre-urban life—in the country, its rhythms and pursuits and traditions. The turn of the seasons, the sure renewal of leaf and crop, flower and festival, the changeless tracks of the stars, gave lyric poetry its inner weather and its images. They were all there, inexhaustibly, to be praised. For centuries the country town was only an enlarged village, London a constellation of villages. The town might draw the ambitious and the vagabond, but it was in the country that the Golden Age must still be imagined, the lyrical age of innocence and love: whether in pastoral or elegy or lyric, the poet went instinctively to nature for metaphors to convey his deepest feelings.

The Industrial Revolution changed the landscape, as Darwin and nineteenth-century science changed the climate of the mind. An industrial society meant living in towns for more and more people, and a progressively less vital contact with nature. Sooner or later, poetry would have to come to terms with this new way of life, or grow obsolete and pass away in a long sigh of nostalgia. Although from the mid-eighteenth century, some poets attempted the industrial subject, by most it was either ignored or deprecated for many years. This was not, in many cases, because they hated it but because they could find no means of handling the industrial scene imaginatively, of responding to it as a potential source of myth or metaphor. For the later Romantics, industry and the growth of towns seemed to presage the death of beauty: the legend of Vulcan and the Cyclops was all very fine, but the beauty of a blast furnace at night went unseen or at any rate unsung by them; it was at once too alien and too real, and most poets prefer their poetry to swim on illusions rather than to founder upon facts.

When the industrial revolution did rouse a spark in the poetic breast, it failed to produce any noticeable furnace of inspiration. Erasmus Darwin towards the end of the eighteenth century celebrated the power of Steam and the benefits it would confer upon humanity:

Soon shall thy arm, Unconquered Steam! afar
Drag the slow barge, or drive the rapid car;
Or on wide-waving wings expanded bear
The flying-chariot through the fields of air.

—a vision rather more dubiously welcomed by Tennyson in 'Locksley Hall'. Thomas Hood regretted the advent of the steamship because it would take the poetic imagery, the romance, out of seafaring (a view sternly reprobated by Kipling's M'Andrew). Ebenezer Elliot was more enthusiastic, latching on to the modern 'Cyclop's dream', going to town with "Watt! and his million-feeding enginery! Steam-miracles of demi-deity!" Wordsworth, in 'Steamboats, Viaducts, and Railways', gave a measured if prolix blessing to the birth of these inventions:

Nor shall your presence, howsoe'er it mar
The loveliness of Nature, prove a bar
To the Mind's gaining that prophetic sense
Of future change, that point of vision, whence . . .

and so on. James Clerk Maxwell, having written his masterly book on electricity and magnetism, could afford to be facetious about the subject in 'Valentine by a Telegraph Clerk to a Telegraph Clerk'; yet this was one of the earliest attempts to use the new scientific data for poetic metaphor:

The tendrils of my soul are twined
With thine, though many a mile apart,
And thine in close-coiled circuits wind
Around the needle of my heart.

As the nineteenth century wore on some poets developed a greater confidence and ease in dealing with this intractable material, a conscious sense that they must do so if they were to speak for their time. E. B. Browning's heroine, Aurora Leigh, declared of poets that "Their sole work is to represent the age/Their age, not Charlemagne's—this live, throbbing

age", and told them they must not, any more than men of
science, shrink from nature's "warts and blains". It was
revolutionary teaching, a hundred years ago, that the ugly,
the seemingly unpoetic, can be material for poetry. But poets
were beginning to learn the lesson—or rather, relearn it.
D. G. Rossetti could really listen to an engine starting from
a railway station "With a short gathered champing of pent
sound." Alexander Smith's poem in praise of Glasgow fetches
a genuine lyrical note from an industrial scene:—

> *The wild Train plunges in the hills,*
> *He shrieks across the midnight rills;*
> *Streams through the shifting glare,*
> *The roar and flap of foundry fires,*
> *That shake with light the sleeping shires . . .*

John Davidson, like Alexander Smith and E. B. Browning
before him, wished poetry to be made, not out of the past
and the long-sanctified poetic subjects only, but from the
urban experience and scientific facts of his own day.

Now this is not difficult for a poet so long as he confines
himself to a descriptive, relatively superficial level. Rossetti's
'A Trip to Paris and Belgium', from which I have quoted a
line, is an occasional poem: he paints landscapes and town-
scapes in it, not attempting more than a versified docu-
mentary: there is none of the intensity of experience which
he conveyed through his poem, 'The Woodspurge'; like most
other nineteenth-century poets, he went to nature for an
image to express the intenseness of feeling. If we want to see
a state of mind profoundly explored through modern images,
we must look at the third section of Eliot's *East Coker*, where
he compares the soul yielding to 'the darkness of God' with
the consciousness of a theatre audience during a change of
scenery, underground travellers in a train that 'stops too long

between stations', and a patient under ether: and all this is
done, not through metaphor, but through an extended simile
of the classical kind.

It is still remarkably difficult to assimilate modern sense-
data and scientific facts into the poetic life of metaphor. This
is partly because they still lack the depth and maturity of
association from which, as plants from compost, poetry is
nourished. What I wrote about the problem thirty years
ago, seems largely true today:

> Scientific data must first be assimilated by the general con-
> sciousness and integrated with the whole environment; then they
> must undergo a further process of digestion in the individual
> poetic organs . . . The key word is 'understanding', imaginative
> comprehension: we cannot be said to understand a thing till we
> have realised it in relation with at least its immediate environ-
> ment, and the poet cannot arrive at this understanding in ad-
> vance of the general consciousness of his age.[9]

To put it in concrete terms: though a poet may use pylons
descriptively, or even for a simile, he will be unlikely to use
them successfully in metaphor until they are no longer alien
to the general consciousness but have become naturalised
objects in man's environment, as telegraph poles *have* become. The passionate fusing of object and idea, which is
metaphor, cannot take place until the object has undergone
this process of assimilation and ceased to be a foreign body.
The same must hold true of scientific theory. Heisenberg's
Principle of Uncertainty, for example, has great relevance to
the problem of creative experiment in poetry; but, until it
has become as much a commonplace of our thinking as the
Principle of Gravity, the poet can use it only for descriptive,
not for metaphorical, purposes.

Another difficulty confronting the poet who wants to use
such modern material is, to put it bluntly, his instinctive dis-

trust of the present. We may smile at the late eighteenth-century's love of ruins, its passion for the Gothic; but we have to notice how, in W. H. Auden's earlier poetry, though it is the life of golf-clubs, bridge-tables, and middle-class neurosis which excites his satire, his lyrical feeling is roused by *abandoned* lead mines, *ramshackle* engines. Here, even in a poet who does full justice to the contemporary scene, the old Romantic Adam is seen at work. Industrial objects long-established or in decay have a lyrical attraction, because they have become part of the landscape, far greater than that of any bright new factory on the Great West Road. And I sus-pect that Auden's poetic obsession in the early Thirties with the middle classes was due far less to any political programme than to the fascination held for him by a way of life at once familiar and, as he believed, in rapid decay.

The contemporary poet unconsciously distrusts the pres-ent, in so far as what it offers him is the life of cities and machines and ever-accelerating material progress—a life that seems to give his poetry such meagre nourishment. Neverthe-les, he must try to make the best of it; and if the reader is historically minded enough to look up the poetry written by my friends and myself during the Thirties, he will see that determined attempts were made to absorb the material set before us. There was a fair amount of lyrical or rhapsodic writing about the urban scene (Spender's 'The Landscape near an Aerodrome: MacNeice's 'Birmingham'). I myself, in sequences such as 'From Feathers to Iron', sought to make metaphors from the machine, and dovetail them with meta-phors from nature. Contrary to accepted belief, there was little directly political poetry; but social criticism pervaded much of the verse we then wrote—and heaven knows the society we lived in gave abundant scope for such criticism: Auden gibed and hammered at its psychological malaise; MacNeice in 'Autumn Journal',[10] the long poem which, of everything we wrote, conveys best the inner and outer weather of those times, attacked our society in straightforward moral terms:

This England is tight and narrow, teeming with unwanted
  Children who are so many, each is alone . . .
Things were different when men felt their programme
  In the bones and pulse, not only in the brain,
Born to a trade, a belief, a set of affections . . .

It is here that, for a few years, the spirit of the Common Muse came into touch again with English poetry. Social criticism—indignation at the folly, cant, or self-seeking of rulers, the apathy or intolerable conditions of the ruled—was the leit-motif of this poetry, as it had once been a stock subject of the broadside ballads. Though we knew our poems would be read in studies, not sung at street corners, we hoped at least that it would have an impact different from that of the ingrown, subjective poetry to which it succeeded. We had, as Wilfred Owen had twenty years before, an urgent and compulsive subject outside ourselves which we felt could invigorate poetry and extend its range. We were under no illusions that we could match the popularity of the broadsides; but we wished our poems to reach out beyond the cliques of the 'poetry-lovers' and the intellectuals. And then the ghost of the Common Muse –for it had only been a shadowy revenant—withdrew; but not without leaving on these poets a mark which could be seen in their writing long after each had gone his own way, following new pre occupations: some may call it a disfigurement but I see it as an honourable scar.

A century ago A. H. Clough, anticipating D. H. Lawrence, wrote in *Dipsychus*, "The age of instinct has, it seems, gone by." He foresees the machine doing our work for us, and us becoming parts of a vast machine in which it may happen that

No individual soul has loftier leave
Than fiddling with a piston or a valve.
Well, one could bear that also . . .

                                        solaced still
By thinking of the leagued fraternity,
And of co-operation, and the effect
Of the great engine. If indeed it work,
And is not a mere treadmill! Which it may be;
Who can confirm it is not so?

In his tentative, open-minded way Clough put forward an
alarming possibility, which for Auden ninety years later has
become a disastrous fact:—

Whichever way we turn, we see
Man captured by his liberty.
The measurable taking charge
Of him who measures . . .

Boys trained by factories for leading
Unusual lives as nurses, feeding
Helpless machines, girls married off
To typewriters, old men in love
With prices they can never get,
Homes blackmailed by a radio set,
Children inherited by slums
And idiots by enormous sums.[11]

'Man captured by his liberty'—to this has come the dream
of the Victorian age, when "a new conception of personal
liberty emerged and the mass of the population of Europe
became free . . . as it had never been free before."[12]

Verse will survive in a materialist society—it is useful for
pop songs and advertisement jingles: poetry, and particularly
lyrical poetry, if it is to survive at all, can only do so by with-
drawing from the life of society, purifying itself, becoming
an esoteric, mandarin ritual: that is one line of argument.

"The age of instinct has, it seems, gone by." In his poem 'The Triumph of the Machine', D. H. Lawrence cries that the machine will never triumph: sooner or later man's instinctual self will revolt against it; the lark which "nests in his heart", the swan that "swims in the marshes of his loins",

all these creatures that cannot die, driven back
into the innermost corners of the soul
will send up the wild cry of despair . . .

even the lambs will stretch forth their necks like serpents,
like snakes of hate, against the man in the machine . . .[13]

and he will be powerless against them.

It is a consoling prospect, maybe; but what are we supposed to do in the meanwhile, and how in fact will this counter-revolution of man's instinctual forces come about? Must we wait for our civilisation to be shattered by hydrogen bombs before we can start again? Edwin Muir, in a fine visionary poem, 'The Horses', imagines a group of survivors, amid dumb radios and dead tractors, witnessing an epiphany —a herd of horses which come to them

Stubborn and shy, as if they had been sent
By an old command to find our whereabouts
And that long-lost archaic comradeship.[14]

But clearly we are not prepared to offer a thousand megadeaths for the sake of redressing the balance between intellect and instinct, and thus making life easier for poets.

And perhaps the outlook is not quite so bad as it seems. It is true that "things were different when men felt their programme in the bones and pulse, not only in the brain": but it is not so evident, if one glances back at history, that things were noticeably better; the Nazis felt their programme in the bones and pulse all right as well as in the brain. Nor, though a man may no longer be "born to a trade, a belief", is he deprived of "a set of affections". He may very well place his affections upon unworthy objects—automobiles, call-girls, pop singers; but there's really nothing new about conformity with one's group. When all is said and done, it is in man's affections that poetry has her deepest root; in the love of order and pattern, the desire for experience, the rhythms of fresh stimulus and familiar routine, the setting of the heart upon another human being; the simple wish to be alive rather than dead, which is the inarticulate man's form of prayer and praise, and which is felt by a poet as the lyrical impulse.

When we consider the products of the Common Muse, and the work of those who have sought to transplant poetry into the soil of cities and machines, we may well fear that by the urban way of life something in man has been diminished and demeaned. And so it has been: the natural dignity, the spontaneous delight of our country-dwelling ancestors, have largely disappeared from urban cultures; the larger our cities grow, the more we seem to lose touch with the sense of human values created by a small community and fortified by a religion. But man has only lived in cities for a blink of time as yet. He has everything to learn about it still. I believe he is adaptable enough to learn it, and thus, reclaiming the territories of his own nature at present lost, possess himself in greater fullness. Patience is needed, and *la sainte impatience* of which Valéry speaks. And by none more than the poet in his work is this paradox proved true.

5. COUNTRY LYRICS

I prefer to use this modest title, 'Country Lyrics', rather than the larger, question-begging one of 'Nature Poetry', because it is more suitable for the work of the two poets I have chosen to represent my theme. John Clare and William Barnes were country-born, country-bred, and pre-eminently lyrical writers: between them, they cover a period of nearly a hundred years — a period during which English nature poetry, in the accepted sense of the words, reached its greatest heights and would soon fall into a decline. Clare was only twenty-three years younger than Wordsworth, Barnes eight years younger than Clare. Both poets went to the English countryside for their subjects and their inspiration.

But, before we come to them, we must inquire into this matter of nature poetry in general—what did it mean, and can it be said to exist at all today? Joseph Warren Beach, in his massive survey, *The Concept of Nature in Nineteenth-Century English Poetry*,[1] says that this concept has all but disappeared from twentieth-century verse, partly because the religious elements in the concept are no longer assumed to be true, partly because modern critical thought rejects the animism which survived in romantic ideas of nature. A contemporary British poet has put it like this:

We may find an image for our own uncircumscribed energies in the sea or the north wind, but we are unlikely to perform sacrifices to Poseidon or Boreas. Sea remains sea for us, and wind remains wind, phenomena of an outside nature, although their mystery and turbulence may make us aware of similar energies in ourselves. Today it is the inward significance which matters, as if the gods had shifted their centre of gravity from the external plane to the inner kingdom of ourselves.[2]

Now this is true enough: but is there not a sense in which it has been true, where lyric poetry is concerned, for a long time? Certainly, when Wordsworth in *Tintern Abbey* and *The Prelude* adapted primitive animistic beliefs to his own sophisticated form of pantheism (the spirit of nature as an active principle) he wrote of nature's forces as *objective* entities, whose behaviour was animated and purposive. But in his lyrics the emphasis is surely changed: the daffodil poem is not a poem about daffodils, but a poem about the state of mind which daffodils set up in him, answered, and explained to him; just as 'The Highland Reaper' is not except superficially a poem about a girl reaping and singing, but uses her to express a mood of his own.

The 'objective correlative' existed a very long time before Mr. Eliot found that name for it. In the *Georgics* Virgil was writing an agricultural textbook: but now and then, as in the passages about spring or the weather signs from Book I, the poem modulates from a didactic tone into a lyrical one; and when this happens, objective though the description may still be, the heightened language makes us aware that the poet's state of mind—of joy, it may be, or wonder, or tenderness—has taken over and is using the natural phenomena which aroused it, to convey his own quickened feelings. It may be true, though it has not been proved, that nature is indifferent to us, neutral: but it is certainly not true, even today, that we are indifferent to nature. The fact of our knowing what atmospheric conditions produce a rainbow, what biological events constitute a rose or an antelope, does not inhibit us from responding to the beauty of such objects,

or render our feelings about them either untrue or un-
necessary.

However uncompromisingly Tennyson spoke of 'brainless
nature', and Housman of 'heartless, witless nature', they
could still give whole-hearted assent to the April violet or
the cherry tree in bloom. However convinced was Hardy by
Darwin's natural selection, and thus of nature as a mindless
power indifferent to man, as a poet he could not deal with
her on such terms: in his experience nature did not *feel*
neutral, but for the most part recalcitrant, capricious, hostile
or cruel in her workings: and so he had to anthropomorphise
the principle of her existence under such guise as the Pur-
blind Doomsters, or the Immanent Will. Many thousands of
generations, after all, have felt a close communion with the
weather, with animals and vegetation. Is it likely that this
deep-rooted association should be grubbed up by a century
or two of scientific knowledge? Is it desirable even? I am in
no way convinced that man's mind is better nourished by a
botanist's definition of a rose than by a poet's description of
its shape and scent, or the love-metaphor he uses it for: nor
can I believe the two are contradictory, or that the one makes
the other invalid. We need them both. To say 'My love is
like a red, red rose' is not to talk nonsense, although no one
but a lunatic could in fact mistake a girl for a rose. I want to
return to this point presently, for it is a critical one. But just
now let us go a bit further afield.

The classical eclogue differs from the sixteenth- or seventeenth-century pastoral in that the writers of the former had
generally a more intimate knowledge of what they were
talking about. Virgil, for instance, knowing from personal
observations the countryman's hard life and the small-
holder's predicament when dispossessed by a war veteran,
toughened the idyllic with the realistic. But behind all pastoral lay a sense, like an ancestral memory, of 'the great, good

place', whether it was mythologised as the Garden of Eden or as the Golden Age—a time and a place in which man was innocent and divinity lived close to him, spoke with him through river, animal and tree. That was the source of nature poetry. In the widest sense, such poetry could be said to range from primitive incantations to Theocritus' Idylls or Catullus praising his beloved Sirmio or Lucretius writing *De Rerum Natura*. But we are concerned at the moment with nature poetry in the strict sense of a poetry rooted in some religious or philosophical concept about nature; so let us turn to English poets of the eighteenth-century. As Mr. Robert Langbaum puts it,

> The religion of nature [in the 18th century] derived from Newton's demonstration that everything from the fall of an apple to the movement of planets is governed by a single law. To people whose Christianity was waning, a nature so orderly seemed to offer new evidence of God's existence and a new source of religious emotion.[3]

This, of course, is a far cry from animism: we must wait for Wordsworth's earlier poetry before we get the full sense of an inter-animation between man and nature. But the philosophical concept of nature has been expressed by Pope in "All are but parts of one stupendous whole", and in such passages as

> *Whate'er of life all quick'ning ether keeps,*
> *Or breathes through air, or shoots beneath the deeps,*
> *Or pours profuse on earth, one nature feeds*
> *The vital flame, and swells the genial seeds.*

In *Windsor Forest* (it is, of course, not nature poetry in our sense, but a mixture of the topographical poem after the tradition of Denham's *Coopers Hill*, and the patriotic idyll) Pope gives us some brilliantly coloured pictures of nature, commends the country life, and glances back to a Golden Age—"The groves of Eden, vanish'd now so long, / Live in description and look green in song". He was perfectly well aware that such verse is partial and artificial: as he said in his *Discourse on Pastoral Poetry*, its virtue lies "in exposing the best side only of a shepherd's life, and in concealing its miseries". Goldsmith's *The Deserted Village* laments the dispossession of a community which sustained something of that Age's mythical simplicity and innocence. Crabbe, too, was writing not about nature as such but about men and women living in country places: his, like Goldsmith's or Pope's, is the classical view of nature—he wants soundness, fertility, not the picturesque for its own sake. Yet, while deprecating a thin or derelict soil, he could be eloquent about it:

> *There poppies nodding mock the hope of toil;*
> *There the blue bugloss paints the sterile soil;*
> *Hardy and high, above the slender sheaf,*
> *The slimy mallow waves her silky leaf;*
> *O'er the young shoots the charlock throws a shade,*
> *And clasping tares cling round the sickly blade;*
> *With mingled tints the rocky coasts abound,*
> *And a sad splendour vainly shines around.*

This objectivity about nature, this non-identification with her, is the normal practice of Augustan poets and of those, like Crabbe, who worked in their tradition. With it went a kind of language, cool, balanced, elegant, whose echoes could still be heard a century and more later. It was Frost, but it could just as well have been Pope or Crabbe, who wrote "Or highway where the slow wheel pours the sand", and "The swarm dilating round the perfect trees". But when Frost said, of an abandoned pile of logs, that it was there "To warm the frozen swamp as best it could/With the slow smokeless burning of decay",[4] while the idiom of the second line is Augustan, the thought of the passage is not: there is a kind of identification with nature here, a touch of the 'pathetic

fallacy', which gives the lines their special imaginative resonance. Though it was Wordsworth who opened up the field,
certain precursors of the Romantics did, as we know, make
tentative approaches to it: Shaftesbury's *Characteristics*
(1711) includes a prose-poem in praise of nature which
might well have served as a source for *Tintern Abbey*: in
Collins, Cowper, Gray, Akenside, Beattie, we can hear pre-
echoes of a sensibility towards nature different from the con-
ceptual attitude of the Augustans—a sensibility which meant
a gradual movement away from the Augustans' more scientific to the Romantics' more religious conceptions, and would
lead the poet towards a deeper and more personal involvement with nature.

This involvement brought in what Ruskin called the
'pathetic fallacy'. Pathetic, in the sense of a transference between natural phenomena and human feelings, it certainly
is: but in what sense is it a fallacy? Can we even be quite
sure it is one? Here I return to the problem with which I
started. A poet talks about "the cruel, crawling, hungry
foam". Well, we may admit that foam, like "the wrinkled
sea", can be said to crawl: but we are quite certain that it is
not a sentient object which is hungry and cruel. But we know
equally well that the poet is talking about the way a stealthy,
incoming, drowning tide affects him. Why need we be out-
raged by what is on the emotional level the same sort of
device as the Latin transferred epithet is on a linguistic level?

The pathetic fallacy is considered a fallacy nowadays because it is a projection of our own moods upon a neutral
screen, upon nature. This view, says Mr. Charles Davy in a
highly suggestive passage,

is held because it accords with a picture of the world that comes
naturally to the onlooker consciousness; and to accept it involves
doing some violence to experience. For even today . . . we do
not *experience* nature as neutral, but as hostile or friendly,

cheerful or melancholy, turbulent or calm. These are some of
nature's 'moods', and in our experience of them there is nothing
to suggest that we have put them there . . . we are always still
able, if we wish, to distinguish nature's moods from our own.[5]

The onlooker consciousness, Mr. Davy argues, being science-
derived, "is always inclined to analyse an experience into
causes and components", a process which "carries us away
from the direct experience". Yet what we experience is still
the shape, colour and scent of a rose, not its biochemistry;
and we should not be so dazzled by science as to assume that
this direct experience is "somehow superficial or even illusory
. . . We are not predisposed by the prestige of science to
assume that, since we know how a book is made and printed,
it can have nothing significant to say; but we are predisposed
to the same kind of assumption about the world of nature".

    I don't think that last analogy will bear close examination.
But, Mr. Davy continues:

When . . . we come to poetry about nature . . . we are inclined
to assume that the poem cannot be making us aware of any
significance inherent in nature, and must therefore be telling us
something about the poet's feelings.
    Of course there are many instances where a poet does use an
'objective correlative' to symbolise human feelings; but why does
this method work? Could it work as well as it does unless nature
itself were symbolic? . . . Hence it need not be a question of
'either-or'—either a projection of the poet's feelings on to a
neutral nature as though onto a blank screen, or nature giving
symbolic expression to some objectively real characteristic of the
universe. When a poet uses images drawn from nature, he may
be taking from nature's symbolic language a phrase which also
expresses something he has himself felt—something which be-
longs to his inner life and is not drawn directly from nature, but
finds a responsive echo there.[6]

If Mr. Davy is talking sense—and I believe he is—a considerable shift in our idea about modern nature poetry should
follow.

Mr. Langbaum sees the subject from a different viewpoint. He believes that certain American poets—Frost, Wallace Stevens and Marianne Moore, for instance—have begun a new nature poetry which does not conflict with the findings of science but is based upon "the exciting new concept, the only one that could inspire conviction . . . that of the mind-lessness of nature, its nonhuman otherness". His examples seem to fall into two categories. On the one hand, there is Marianne Moore's poem 'A Grave',[7] which she opens by telling us that "she will render the sea not from the human point of view, but as it is in itself". As I read the poem, it is a good description of the sea, with no human emotions involved, but still (and inevitably) described "from the human point of view". At the end, Miss Moore places the cautionary lines, ". . . looking as if it were not that ocean in which dropped things are bound to sink—/In which if they turn and twist, it is neither with volition nor consciousness". All she is doing, in effect, is to say that things are not what they seem; as Frost does in his poem about the burnt-out farmhouse ("One had to be versed in country things/Not to believe the phoebes wept"[8]). It is salutary to be reminded that natural objects do not have human purposiveness or feel-ings; but I do not see that such reminders constitute a new nature poetry.

On the other hand, Mr. Langbaum adduces Wallace Stevens' 'The Snowman', "which contrasts the inevitably anthropomorphic human apprehension of a landscape with the landscape as it might be apprehended by the mindless 'mind' of a snow man". I have studied this poem very atten-tively, and come to the conclusion that the poet is attempting the impossible. He has tried to put himself into the mind, not even of an animal, but of an artifact—a snow man which has no sentience whatsoever. Mr. Langbaum's "as it *might be* apprehended" gives the game away: the poet has sought by this means to convey the absolute purity, the essence, of a winter landscape; but his method is not purely objective. Side-stepping the pathetic fallacy, he has tumbled into another pitfall—let us call it the noetic fallacy.

It is a relief to emerge from these turbid waters onto dry land, an English countryside. "I found the poems in the fields," said John Clare; and again, "I wrote because it pleased me in sorrow, and when happy it makes me happier." He wrote a very great deal of poetry, in his young days when he was relatively cheerful and through the later years of solitude as an inmate of Northampton Asylum: even here, many of the poems had their roots in the fields; for what he cherished was "the power of words to prolong and renew that rapture which he felt in the presence of nature."[9] This hyperaesthesia he shared with the young Keats, born two years after him; but he did not share Keats' wish to be 'philosophical', and said of the other poet, "He often described Nature as she appeared to his fancies, and not as he would have described her had he witnessed the things he described." Clare's poetry has no designs on us, in the sense that he is content to show and praise country things without moralising overmuch about nature or conceptualising her. He poured the stuff out: a friend wrote prophetically, when Clare was twenty-seven,

It is to be greatly feared that the man will be afflicted with insanity if his talent continues to be forced as it has been these four months past; he has no other mode of easing the fever that oppresses him after a tremendous fit of rhyming except by getting tipsy.[10]

Clare is, in fact, the very type of a lyric poet.

He was a peasant lad, largely self-taught. His early poems show, as we would expect, the influence of eighteenth-century nature poetry. 'Helpstone' is a miniature 'Deserted

Village': the famous passage about the snail has, in its first
version, a strong rhythmical resemblance to Collins' 'Ode
to Evening'—

> *Jet-black and shining, from the dripping hedge*
> *Slow peeps the fearful snail,*
>   *And from each tiny bent*
>   *Withdraws his timid horn.*

This has a precision and minutenes, though, which is foreign
to the earlier poet of "Or where the beetle winds / His small
but sullen horn". 'Ode to Evening' is an exquisitely wrought
poem. In the Augustan way, it uses Personification—a device by which such poets aimed to distance a poem from the
specific experience that prompted it, and to generalise the
particular. When, some years later, Clare rewrote the stanza
I have quoted, he made this—

> *And note on hedgerow baulks, in moisture sprent,*
>   *The jetty snail creep from the mossy thorn,*
> *With earnest heed and tremulous intent,*
>   *Frail brother of the morn,*
> *That from the tiny bents and misted leaves*
>   *Withdraws his timid horn,*
>   *And fearful vision weaves.*

About this we might say that there is an over-accumulation
of epithets, and that "Frail brother of the morn" is more
Collins-like than anything in the first version, whereas "And
fearful vision weaves" is more romantic—how romantic is
easily seen if we compare it with Collins' "Thy dewy fingers
draw / The gradual dusky veil". But the point is that Clare's
second version, apart from the fourth line, remains very
nearly as objective as his first: it still gives an accurate description of how a snail moves, the poet's emotion brushing
it with only the lightest touch, if at all.

In his earlier poetry, Clare seldom tried to burden nature with his own emotions. But his experience was worked deep into the verse, so that we are aware of personal feeling below its surface, flavouring the whole: for example, in the passage from *The Shepherd's Calendar* where the shepherd's boy looks up, as Clare must often have looked, at a March sky:

While, far above, the solitary crane
Swings lonely to unfrozen dykes again,
Cranking a jarring, melancholy cry
Through the wild journey of the cheerless sky.

Nothing of the pathetic fallacy here. Nevertheless such heightened passages tell their tale, in Clare's pastoral as they do in Virgil's Georgic. However distanced from the final poem, emotion set up by imperative experience will create poetry of a special resonance. 'Solitary', 'jarring, melancholy cry', 'cheerless', are objectively precise; but also they tell us something about the poet's state of mind: he had little contact with the writers of his day, few people he could talk with on equal terms at home: this solitude was to thicken into the isolation of the melancholic in his asylum: and far beneath "Swings lonely to *unfrozen* dykes again", can we not hear a cry for human warmth, human companionship?

The companionship with nature was not enough. To what extent Clare was a solitary as a child, I cannot determine: in some of his poems he tells us that he was, but others speak of the happy games and pursuits he took part in with companions; no doubt, like the young Hardy of "Swift as the light, / I flew my fairy flight: / Ecstatically I moved, and feared no night",[11] he had moods of gregariousness, and moods of preferring his own company: regret for lost childhood is a common subject throughout his verse. But certainly as a man, even before madness overcame him, Clare was lonely. A close acquaintance with intellectual equals, writers in particular, would have given him greater resource, self-criticism, self-knowledge even, as a poet; might have discouraged him from such errors as addressing a glow-worm, "Tasteful illumination of the night", and given a firmer bone-structure to his verse. For his longer poems, with the exception of *The Shepherd's Calendar*, tend to monotony and repetitiveness: sometimes they read like versified catalogues or nature-notes, so that the poem, instead of coming to a resolution, merely comes to a stop, as if Clare could for the moment think of nothing more to say. We have noticed this same lack of economy and finish in the street ballads. In Clare's enormous output, there is a good deal which does not rise above the level of album verse, giving us agreeable pictures of nature, conventional sentiments, a perfunctory touch of moralising, but little more. This is the provincial side of him. The conversation of fellow poets, when he was a young man, might well have tempered with criticism and judgment the exuberance of his talent—a muse he found so ecstatic and consoling in the practice that he failed to realise how much she wanted to be disciplined.

But, had he learnt from others such organization and correctness, I fancy more would have been lost than gained. We should not have the down-to-earth, unconventional, forthright quality we get in such phrases as "the clod-brown lark", "daisies button into buds", "the giggling of the brook", "the jaundice-tinctured primrose", "The restless heat seems twittering by", "The plopping guns' sharp, momentary shock." Nor should we find those dialect words which flavour a passage that might have been insipid without them—'fluskering', 'swaliest', 'drowking', 'water-pudge', 'gleg', 'soodles', 'blea', 'crimpling', and hundreds more.

Nor am I at all convinced that a greater degree of sophistication, though it might have extended the range of Clare's subjects, would have deepened his treatment of them. He was interested in what lay about him—birds, flowers, beasts, fish, insects; the turn of the seasons, and the changing looks of nature; the solitary places, and the landscape with figures; the countryman's pursuits, hardships, and pleasures: and a saving instinct confined him to such things—these, and the promptings of his own heart, which were too sincere to admit the grandiose. Even when he refers to the Chain of Being, in his verses 'On a Lost Greyhound', he does so without pomp or pretension:—

> For dogs, as men, are equally
> A link of nature's chain,
> Form'd by that hand that formed me,
> Which formeth naught in vain.

His indignation, again, is kept for things that affect him and his neighbours immediately—cruelty to animals (for they were his neighbors too); the poverty and the decay of old customs brought about by enclosures of the land. Long poems, such as 'The Parish', show that Clare could turn his indignation to effective satire; but they lack the narrative momentum which Crabbe brought to a similar subject.

I said that Clare is the very type of a lyric poet. The most compelling passages in his longer poems are lyrical; the most memorable of the shorter are almost all lyrics. The cowslip attracts his eye, as cowslips did twenty years before, when he was a child;

> But I'm no more akin to thee,
> A partner of the spring;
> For time has had a hand with me,
> And left an alter'd thing:
>
> A thing that's lost thy golden hours,
> And all I witness'd then,
> Mix'd in a desert, far from flowers,
> Among the ways of men.

The poem in which this stanza occurs was one of those written at Helpstone between 1821 and 1824. After 1824, J. W. Tibble tells us, "he wrote no more narrative and few long descriptive poems; his work became essentially lyrical".[12] That stanza from 'To a Cowslip' gives the quality of Clare's lyric: it is limpid and sincere, saved from any facile or sentimental regret by the unillusioned hardness of the third and fourth lines.

Earlier, Clare had written charming lyrics, such as 'Patty of the Vale' or 'My love's like a lily', which have the innocence of folksong, and one or two poems—'Dolly's Mistake', for example—which show an obvious affinity with the street-ballad. We may regret it that Clare spent so much of his earlier years in long descriptive and narrative poems, and did not more often tap the pure lyric source within him, or the folksong idiom which was there to his hand. It is sad that the lyric impulse could not be fully realised until he himself was confined in Northampton Asylum—the impulse which produced this, for example:

Peggy said good morning and I said goodbye,
When farmers dib the corn and laddies sow the rye.
Young Peggy's face was commonsense and I was rather shy
When I met her in the morning when the farmers sow the rye.

Her half-laced boots fit tightly as she tripped among the grass,
And she set her foot so lightly where the early bee doth pass.
Oh, Peggy was a young thing, her face was commonsense,
I courted her about the spring and loved her ever since.

Oh, Peggy was the young thing and bonny as to size;
Her lips were cherries of the spring and hazel were her eyes.
Oh, Peggy she was straight and tall as is the poplar tree,
Smooth as the freestone of the wall, and very dear to me.

Oh, Peggy's gown was chocolate and full of cherries white;
I keep a bit on't for her sake and love her day and night.
I drest myself just like a prince and Peggy went to woo,
But she's been gone some ten years since, and I know not what
     to do.

This, to me, is a test poem. If any student of English
literature failed to respond to it, I would advise him to take
up some other course: if I heard a teacher or critic dismissing
it, or adopting a supercilious attitude towards it, I would
wish to have him instantly deprived of his post. It is a test
poem, because we can only accept it on its own terms and
at its own level—one of those pure lyrics, like 'O Westron
wind', which, coming straight from the heart, must go
straight to the heart, and which evaporate if we stop and
question it on the frontier: we get nothing more from it, as
we do from Wordsworth's *Lucy* poems, say, by 'close reading': if we interpose a cerebral filter between us and such
phrases as "Peggy's face was commonsense" or "Smooth as
the freestone of the wall", we merely deny ourselves the
poem's effective quality without enriching or enlarging its
meaning. To feel it as it should be felt entails an act of
joyful submission. Such an act of submission may be difficult
for a modern reader, habituated by the earnestness or offi-
ciousness of literary critics to believe that no poem is worth-
while unless a fine dust of footnotes can be beaten out of
it. But if the reader cannot make this surrender to simple
poetry, his mastery of more complex kinds will be a little
suspect, for it means that his channel to poetry's source has
become clogged.

'Peggy' is a minor poem, no doubt; but the minor lyric
offers a test none the less valuable for being elementary: it
tests the spontaneity, the naturalness, of our response to
poetry. If our reaction is positive, we have the root of the

matter in us. During his last twenty years, the best of Clare's poems were stripped down to essentials, reduced to a crystal, child-like sincerity, which reminds us of some of Blake's lyrics. It was Clare, but it could just as well be Blake, who wrote in 'The Dying Child',

> *Infants, the children of the spring!*
>   *How can an infant die*
> *When butterflies are on the wing,*
>   *Green grass, and such a sky?*
>   *How can they die at spring?*

Or again, we can hear Blake in the second and third stanzas of 'I lost the love of heaven', just as we can hear Emily Brontë in its first and fourth:—

> *I lost the love of heaven above,*
>   *I spurned the lust of earth below,*
> *I felt the sweets of fancied love,*
>   *And hell itself my only foe.*

> *I lost earth's joys, but felt the glow*
>   *Of heaven's flame abound in me,*
> *Till loveliness and I did grow*
>   *The bard of immortality.*

> *I loved, but woman fell away;*
>   *I hid me from her faded flame.*
> *I snatched the sun's eternal ray*
>   *And wrote till earth was but a name.*

> *In every language upon earth,*
>   *On every shore, o'er every sea,*
> *I gave my name immortal birth*
>   *And kept my spirit with the free.*

We remember the passion for freedom which animated Emily Brontë. Freedom, Mr. Tibble tells us, is a clue to an

understanding of Clare's asylum poetry: "The significance
lies not in his longing for freedom—the asylum was always
'prison' to him—but in his achievement of that freedom in
his verses. The price of freedom was a disassociation of the
man and the poet."[13] I am not quite sure that I know what
that last phrase means. Many of the asylum poems, it is
true, though by no means all of them, are impersonal to a
degree we rarely find in the earlier work. Clare's madness
does seem to have caused his poetry to break through to a
deeper imaginative level—one at which, as in the poem I
have just read, hallucination takes on the compelling gran-
deur of vision; while, in such a lyric as 'Peggy', we recognise
the peculiar flavour and felicity of unpremeditated art. But
Clare's guiding themes did not alter—the heart's affections,
the love of woman and of country things. They come together, out of Clare's crazed mind, in a lyric of the most
exquisite rhythm and character and purity:—

> Love, meet me in the green glen,
>   Beside the tall elm tree,
> Where the sweetbrier smells so sweet agen;
>   There come with me,
>   Meet me in the green glen.

> Meet me at the sunset
>   Down in the green glen,
> Where we've often met
>   By hawthorn-tree and foxes' den,
>   Meet me in the green glen.

> Meet me in the green glen,
>   By sweetbrier bushes there;
> Meet me by your own sen,
>   Where the wild thyme blossoms fair,
>   Meet me in the green glen.

Meet me by the sweetbrier,
  By the mole-hill swelling there;
When the west glows like a fire
God's crimson bed is there.
  Meet me in the green glen.

I would like to set beside that poem of Clare's a lyric written by William Barnes after his wife's death: he puts it into the mouth and language of a Dorset peasant. 'The Wife A-Lost' has nothing in common with Clare's poem except lyric sincerity, a use of refrain, and the country life.

Since I noo mwore do zee your feäce,
  Up steäirs or down below,
I'll zit me in the lwonesome pleäce
  Where flat-bough'd beech do grow;
Below the beeches' bough, my love,
  Where you did never come,
An' I don't look to meet ye now,
  As I do look at hwome.

Since you noo mwore be at my zide,
  In walks in zummer het,
I'll goo alwone where mist do ride,
  Drough trees a- drippèn wet:
Below the rain-wet bough, my love,
  Where you did never come,
An' I don't grieve to miss ye now,
  As I do grieve at hwome.

Since now bezide my dinner-bwoard
  Your väice do never sound,
I'll eat the bit I can avword
  A-vield upon the ground;
Below the darksome bough, my love,
  Where you did never dine,
An' I don't grieve to miss ye now,
  As I at hwome do pine.

Since I do miss your väice an' feäce
  In präyer at eventide,
I'll praÿ wi' woone sad väice vor greäce
  To goo where you do bide;
Above the tree an' bough, my love,
  Where you be gone avore,
An' be a wäitèn vor me now
  To come vor evermwore.

The pattern is simple, the feeling true: a bereaved husband will frequent places that do not remind him of his loneliness, as the home does. The poem is relieved by this realism from any touch of mawkishness, as it is aerated all through by its musicality.

Like Clare, Barnes had the gift for simplicity—for the language of the heart. Like Clare, he was country-born and bred, the son of a small farmer in the Blackmore Vale of Dorset. He left school at thirteen and taught himself that remarkable variety of skills which was to make him one of the most learned men of his time. He was a prolific poet, like Clare, but more consistently a lyric one: they shared the same accuracy of observation; and each, though previously unknown in the cultivated world, had a great success with his first book. But here the ways part. William Barnes was a many-sided man, full of intellectual curiosity, a competent engraver, a skilful amateur musician, interested in folklore and scientific subjects; for many years he kept a school of his own, first at Mere in Wiltshire, then at Dorchester; as a schoolmaster he was a hundred years ahead of his time in the enlightenment and humaneness he brought to education. During this long period of teaching in small provincial schools, Barnes taught himself no less than sixty languages, western and oriental, in order to pursue his study of philology.

There can be little doubt that this passion for philology turned his mind to the use of dialect in his own poems. He believed that the Blackmore Vale dialect, familiar to him from childhood, was not a corruption of standard English but a pure form of language—a distinct branch of Anglo-Saxon speech—eminently suitable for poetry. Barnes carried his love of linguistic purity, his dislike of Latin, Greek, or French derivations, to a point sometimes of pedantic eccentricity; and it may surprise us that the poetry he wrote in dialect should show so little trace of the artificiality we might expect from an enterprise so apparently *voulu* and premeditated. But we must remember that he was only making a conscious exploration of a language native to him. Introducing his *Poems of Rural Life*, Barnes wrote,

The Dorset dialect is a broad and bold shape of the English language as the Doric was of the Greek . . . and altogether as fit a vehicle of rustic feeling and thought as the Doric is found in the Idyllia of Theocritus.

The writer's intention, he declared, is

to utter the happy emotions with which his mind can dwell on the charms of rural nature and the better feelings and more harmless joys of the small farm house and happy cottage.

Barnes was not ignorant, however, of the darker and seamier side of rural life, nor unmoved by it: no less than Clare he was angered by the enclosure system which increased its poverty, just as he was by the exploitation of labour in industry: social injustices suffered by the land-workers were the subject of Eclogues he wrote during the Thirties.

Like another poet-parson, George Herbert, Barnes possessed a great goodness and simplicity of heart, which steadied the course of a versatile intellect. It is this quality which, informing his poems, gives them their special innocence, whether of gaiety or sadness; and it was this quality, in his poems and himself, that endeared him to Dorset folk, who still talk of William Barnes with a personal affection as though he had died, not eighty years ago, but yesterday.

Although he seldom read contemporary verse and preferred seclusion to any close contact with the literary world of his day, ("Half hermit, half enchanter," Kilvert called him) Barnes' poetry was highly esteemed by fellow poets. Tennyson and Arnold admired it; Palgrave lectured on it from the Oxford Chair of Poetry; Patmore felt a special sympathy for his work, and said "His writings have all the qualities of— classics . . . He has done a small thing well, while his contemporaries have been mostly engaged in doing big things ill." Gerard Manley Hopkins studied Barnes' methods—his experiments, for instance, in patterns of internal assonance —and wrote that in his dialect poems "there is more true poetry than there is in Burns; I do not say, of course, vigour or passion or humour or a lot of things, but the soul of poetry."

But why is it that Barnes' dialect poems are superior to the very considerable number he wrote in standard English? Compare 'The Wife A-Lost' with another poem written about his dead Julia: here is the fourth stanza of it, which says very much the same things as are said in the dialect poem:—

> How can I live my lonesome days?
> How can I tread my lonesome ways?
> How can I take my lonesome meal?
> Or how outlive the grief I feel?
> Or how again look on the weal?
> Or sit at rest, before the heat
> Of winter fires to miss thy feet,
> When evening light is waning?

The feeling behind it is no less keen; but it is insipid, characterless, abstract, lacking in musical resonance, compared with 'The Wife A-Lost'. We may say that, in the latter, the poet was enabled to distance his feeling by uttering it through the speech of a country labourer: this, I think, is true; yet it does not explain why Barnes' standard-English poems, which have no strong personal feeling behind them, are still inferior to dialect ones on comparable subjects.

I said earlier that "by writing in their language, Barnes tapped the Dorset countryman's simpleness of mind and drew from it the sturdiness and innocence which give his dialect poetry its specific charm." Innocence was perhaps the wrong word here—he had no need to go outside himself for that; 'unsophistication' would be a better one, for this was a quality to which, in spite of his wide intellectual interests, he always responded. On the other hand, we must not confuse unsophistication with artlessness when we consider his poetry. A friend and fellow-Dorsetman, Thomas Hardy, wrote this of Barnes' dialect poems:

> Barnes . . . really belonged to the literary school of such poets as Tennyson, Gray, and Collins, rather than to that of the old unpremeditating singers in dialect. Primarily spontaneous, he was academic closely after; and we find him warbling his native wood-notes with a watchful eye on the predetermined score . . .[14]

Hardy adds the interesting notion that Barnes was saved from "the passion for form"—from a possible tendency to over-indulge his liking for technical experiment and perfection—"by the conditions of his scene, characters, and vocabulary . . . It may have been, indeed, that he saw this tendency in himself, and retained the dialect as a corrective . . ." I myself prefer this view of Hardy's to Mr. Geoffrey Grigson's opinion that Barnes' writing in dialect was a "learned perversity": good poems are not achieved out of learned perversities: Frédéric Mistral, a near-contemporary of Barnes, wrote his finest poetry in the Provençal dialect.

Let us take a look now at Barnes' lyric character. The first things we may notice are the freshness and buoyancy, the use of primary colours—those of nature and those of the

heart; in these lines from 'May', for instance, with their faint
echo of the opening lines of Lucretius:—

> *Mother o' blossoms, and ov all*
> *That's feäir a-vield from Spring till Fall,*
> *The gookoo over white-weäv'd seas*
> *Do come to zing in thy green trees,*
> *An' buttervlees, in giddy flight,*
> *Do gleäm the mwost by thy gaÿ light.*

(It was emigrants, from Dorchester, England, who founded
Dorchester, Massachusetts, and brought that word 'Fall' with
them.) As Lucretius peeps out there, so does Virgil emerge
in some of Barnes' Eclogues—for instance, 'The Common
A-Took In', with its theme of dispossession—or in occasional passages such as

> *An' when by moonlight darksome sheädes*
> *Do lie in grass wi' dewy bleädes,*
> *An' worold-hushen night do keep*
> *The proud an' angry vast asleep . . .*

But the language throughout is Barnes' own, fresh, musical,
homely, consistent, almost never attempting even the
modest heights represented by those last two lines. Because
he was pre-eminently a writer of lyric, we find no arresting
phrase, no profound image—nothing which would dam the
musical flow of the poem. He may bring in a simple, religious moral, as he did when preaching to his country
parishioners: but both his moralising and his sentiment are
all of-a-piece with the lyric simplicity of the poem, seldom
obtruding themselves, finding some natural picture that em-
bodies rather than illustrates them:

> *Though time do dieve me on, my mind*
> *Do turn in love to thee behind,*
> *The seäme's a bullrush that's a-shook*
> *By wind a-blowen up the brook;*

The curlen stream would dreve en down,
But plaÿsome äir do turn 'en roun',
An' meäke en seem to bend wi' love
To zunny hollows up above.

Though the climate of Barnes' verse is mild ("An gi'e me
vaïces that do speak / So soft an' meek, to souls alwone"),
its air is not insipid: the dialect gives it a robustness; the
poet's attentive eye for the detail of his landscape and the
nature of the indigenous figures who work and play and love
therein—this keeps his feet on the ground, keeps the poems
from flying off into grandiose abstraction.

Their basic metre is the four-stress line, varied sometimes
with shorter ones; and this, we have seen, is the staple of
English lyric. There is a constant use of refrain:—

O spread ageän your leaves an' flow'rs
Lwonesome woodlands! Zunny woodlands!
Here underneath the dewy show'rs
O' warm-äir'd spring-time, zunny woodlands!
As when, in drong or open ground,
Wi' happy bwoyish heart I vound
The twitt'ren birds a-builden round
Your high-bough'd hedges, zunny woodlands!

Like Clare's, Barnes' is often a retrospective stance; but he
imparts to it a cordial rather than a melancholy or regretful
tone, partly because of his firm Christian belief, partly because his temperament was more sanguine than Clare's,
partly through the depersonalising nature of lyric and dialect.

Barnes—and this is surprising in so accomplished a techni-
cian—rarely attempted rhythmic variation on the staple
four-stress iambic line. But there is one variant we should
look at, used in 'The Mead A-Mow'd', 'The Welshnut Tree',
and 'The Clote': this is a drifting, surging rhythm, particularly suited to the subject of the Clote (Dorset for water-
lily), whose opening stanzas run as follows:—

O zummer clote! when the brook's a-gliden
  So slow an' smooth down his zedgy bed,
Upon thy broad leaves so seäfe a-riden
  The water's top wi' thy yellow head,
    By alders' heads, O,
    An' bulrush beds, O'
Thou then dost float, goolden zummer clote!

The grey-bough'd withy's a-leänen lowly
  Above the water thy leaves do hide;
The benden bulrush, a-swaÿen slowly,
  Do skirt in zummer thy river's zide;
    An' perch in shoals, O,
    Do vill the holes, O,
Where thou dost float, goolden zummer clote!

It is certainly one of Barnes' finest poems. Yet, to my ear, the refrain is not perfectly satisfactory: its internal rhyme ('float', 'clote'), gives the effect of splitting the final line into a pair of two-stress lines, like the two preceding ones; and to me this effect hurries and narrows the rhythm, which should slow and broaden at this point, making the close of each stanza a little more obtrusive, a little less conclusive, than the ear expects from what has preceded it.

I think Barnes could also be faulted for a certain clumsiness in his use of refrain. One often gets the impression that he thought of the refrain first (many of his poems indeed have the refrain line as their title), and then directed the course of the stanzas too obviously so as to arrive at it from several directions. A refrain in a song lyric, while musically decisive, avoids any weight of poetic meaning: Barnes, though an accomplished musician, did not write his lyrics for music; so their refrains lack the conviction which a tune could give them. It is worth noticing how the refrain of 'My Orcha'd in Linden Lea', set to music by Vaughan Williams, at once justifies itself by reason of the tune— "An' there

vor me the apple tree / *Do leän down low in Linden Lea.*"
In general, this type of alliterative, assonantal refrain, which
Barnes borrowed from Welsh poetry, sounds too artificial:
I don't care for such lines as "Vor Ellen Brine ov Allenburn"
or "But Meäry's smile, o' Morey's Mill", or "Ah! well-a-day!
O well adieu", or "Vrom Paladore—O Polly dear".

Such devices are mostly found in Barnes' second and
third collections of dialect poems, where the lyric spontaneity has become a little jaded, and art sometimes fails
to conceal art. There is a lot of truth in Hardy's remark
about Barnes' keeping "a watchful eye on the predetermined
score": and it must also be said that, in presenting his poems
through the dialect and persona of a Dorset peasant, Barnes
threw into dangerously high relief such sophisticated technical turns as he employed. The internal rhyme, for instance,
of " 'An zoo, when winter skies do *lour,* / An' when the
Stour's a-rollen wide"—an old Irish device; the double cross-
rhymes of "We then mid *yearn* to clim' the *height,* / Where
thorns be *white,* above the *vern*":—the effect is musical
indeed, but because the lines purport to come from a simple
rustic source, the sophisticated rhyming seems a shade in-
congruous, calling attention to itself, to a degree that it would
not do if it came from either an undisguised 'literary' poet
or a professional bard.

So there they are, the two provincials, morbid Clare and
wholesome Barnes, having well-nigh nothing in common—
tradition nor idiom nor fortune nor temperament—nothing
but the need to celebrate a bit of countryside and the con-
tentment they found in so doing: what Palgrave said about
Barnes could largely be applied to Clare as well:

. . . he does not, with the Greeks, treat nature as the outward
manifestation of divine or half-divine existence. She appears,
rather, as a sort of unconscious reflex of human life. The land-

scape of each season, in its turn, seems, indeed, to Barnes to be the genuine echo of our emotions; but it is an echo only; our hearts have, as it were, supplied Nature with the answer which she gives back to us. Yet this echo is so close and dear to the rural poet's mind, that the landscape is always intertwined in his verse with its dominant human interests.

If we study carefully the implications of that passage, we may well find ourselves changing our minds, not about Barnes or Clare, but about nature poetry in general, and its possibilities for the poet today; a poetry neither at the mercy of any pathetic fallacy, as Clare and Barnes were not, nor reduced to something absolutely alien which the poet must approach, if at all, not as a poet but as a scientist. For Clare and Barnes, it is enough to say that they were able to achieve what they did achieve because as poets they were rooted in one place and one subject. It is genius alone which enables a subject to be transplanted to a different place, a later time, and to flourish there. Of that genius, Clare and Barnes had a small but sufficient share.

6. THE GOLDEN BRIDLE

One of the tasks set the mythical heroes of antiquity was the taming of Pegasus. For a whole day Bellerophon pursued the winged horse over Helicon, the home of the Muses. An expert horse-tamer, he exercised all his skill, speed and endurance; but always Pegasus eluded him, mocking him sometimes by allowing him to come close with his halter, then at the last moment spreading its wings and sailing over Bellerophon's head. At the end of the day, the hero lay down exhausted on the hillside and went to sleep. He dreamed that the goddess Athene gave him a golden bridle. When he awoke next morning, he saw a golden bridle lying in the grass beside him—and Pegasus stood there too, submissive, head bowed to receive the bridle, waiting for Bellerophon to mount.

That legend is an image of the creative process, not only in the arts but in the sciences too: there are many cases of scientific problems being resolved when the conscious mind is asleep or engaged elsewhere—the mathematician Poincaré finding the solution of a problem as he stepped into a cab thinking of other matters; Kekulé, riding on a bus and suddenly seeing the carbon and hydrogen atoms join hands to form a chain, and later seeing them in a dream dance round to join hands again, thus discovering the benzene ring. With our own human problems, how often we are told to 'sleep on it'. But we have to play an active part first. Kekulé and

Poincaré would not have received their solutions at all, had they not put in a tremendous amount of conscious work on the problems. Bellerophon would not have been granted the bridle if he had not spent all his energy and skill attempting to catch Pegasus: we may even imagine the golden bridle as a magical object woven out of all his complex, unavailing manoeuvres.

But what is most important is the way he came by it. It was a gift from the goddess. Why is it that in one poem a good poet can capture the inspiration and go soaring up on it, whereas the next poem he writes, though as much skill and energy have gone to it, never leaves the ground? That mythical bridle represents something given, gratuitous—a moment, if you like, of grace—grace which cannot be counted on and in a sense cannot even be earned: it can only be received, though it will certainly never come unless the poet has used all his art, strenuously and truthfully, to deserve it. To change the metaphor, he must work to make his offering acceptable: but whether the god enters into it, whether the sacrifice catches fire of its own accord on the altar—this is beyond the poet's control.

I am not arguing for a divine source of poetic inspiration, nor certainly would I dare to argue against it. All I am saying is that we do not know what transforms good verse into poetry: all we know is that its source appears to lie somewhere in the unconscious; and this is especially true for those *données*, those given lines or phrases which come into the poet's head, sometimes signalling that a new poem is on its way, sometimes altering the course of a poem on which he has already embarked, but always possessing for him a mysterious and potent significance. He must question them deeply, for they may prove to be impostors; if their credentials still hold good, he lets them breed. But of course the two problems are not consecutive: the making of a poem

and the questioning of it during its composition, the creative
and the critical, are two inseparable modes of the one process: every line—even those peremptory 'given' lines that
come out of the blue—has to be judged finally by the poem
as a whole. Here again the golden bridle offers a valid metaphor. A bridle both refrains energy and releases it, disci-
plines and directs: there are times (and these tend to come
in the early stage of composition, I find) when a poet must
exercise stern control lest the poem run away with him; there
are times when he can let the reins lie loose.

The nearer a poem comes to lyric, the greater his need
for this bridle and the more skilful must be his use of it,
for in a sense it is the only control he has. With a narrative
poem, for example, the story, having chosen the general
course, helps to direct it; the same with satire; the modern
'lyrical' poem, so far as it depends upon complexity of structure and irony of meaning, possesses certain built-in checks
on the movement of its language. A pure lyric, on the other
hand, can go in any direction it likes—theoretically, at least
—with nothing to sustain or guide it but its own essential
nature. I do not mean that a lyric has to be meaningless, or
to lack all prose content: what does seem clear is that its
value depends less upon the value of its prose meaning than
does that of any other kind of verse. For this reason, when
the lyric is divorced from the music which supplied it with
momentum and in a sense its *raison d'être*, poets must learn
from the medium itself how to educe a 'singing line'. It is
not primarily a matter of discipline: what Roy Campbell
wrote about certain South African novelists can be applied
just as well to many poets of our time—"They use the snaffle
and the curb all right, / But where's the bloody horse?"[1] We
come nearer if we say it's a matter of "complete truth to
feeling".

In a lyric, the singing line must be unbroken, the poem
all of a piece. If we break the line, inserting snatches of irony

or of rhapsody, or bits of self-conscious commentary, the lyric impulse leaks away: the result is a mixed poem, which may be excellent in its own genre, or may be just another piece of low-pressure verse. In either case, there will not be the *lyric's* "complete truth to feeling", which implies purity or singleness of feeling—and of feeling so compulsive that the poet has no need to argue or comment or be clever about it. I am inclined to think that our failure in the lyric today is largely a failure of nerve: we cannot commit ourselves absolutely to those simple feelings which are the essence of lyric poetry: in mid-air, we begin to wonder whether the bloody horse is there, so we let the poem down—gracefully or with a bump—which is no way to treat Pegasus. To put it another way, a poet writing a lyric is a man flying, not a powered aircraft, but a glider: he depends upon elemental forces in his own mind, as the glider pilot depends on up-draughts and cloud formations, to support him and advise him on his course.

During the last three decades, we have seen violent swings of the pendulum in British poetry. The Forties, reacting from the Thirties, produced a dominant strain of romantic and rhapsodic verse: the Fifties, reacting from Dylan Thomas, sought to deflate their predecessors' emotionalism and false poeticism (as they felt it to be), and write verse of formal elegance, good sense, astringent irony. As John Press remarks in his study of British poetry since the War,[a] the former group "reveal . . . the characteristic vices of Dionysian poetry: a lack of earthiness, sinewy vigour, and plain good sense; a posturing in the role of the artist as seer"; whereas with the latter, he suggests, "irony is often an elegant form of evasion, a defensive gesture to conceal the absence of deep feeling". I do not want to involve myself in this latest outbreak of Apollonian-Dionysian warfare, which tramples over the lyric territory with little regard for such peasants there as only wish for a decent harvest and a quiet life. All I would say is that the love-poem, the most fruitful type of lyric, tends to get ignored or blasted by both sides. The new Dionysian treats his love as a sort of trampoline off which he can bounce higher and higher into a verbal empyrean; the new Apollonian treats his with the scepticism of an immigration officer grilling a suspected plague-carrier.

To write a good lyric of love today, the poet must have surrendered to the feeling of love and been possessed by it. The surrender must be so complete that his sophistication is, for the time being, stripped away and he is nakedly confronted by the most primitive and powerful force in human experience; it will be fatal if he sees this force in the light of its universality—as the world's largest emotional cliché—and therefore tries compromise, cleverness, or evasion. Aphrodite is not to be played about with. Other kinds of poetry may legitimately question her, moralise on her, elaborate, annotate or dress her up: the lyric may do no such thing, for the feeling whose complete truth it must convey is a primary feeling, which self-consciousness can only muddy and dialectic refinements distort. Before he writes a lyric, the poet must have accepted Aphrodite's commonplace, divine illusion—that he and the beloved are unique, that none ever loved before but thou and I. Once he has committed himself absolutely thus, a poet can go on to find many states of mind, many levels of meaning, which may be compassed within the lyric medium. I shall turn now to a few examples from our own time: they are love poems, and they compel us to think again if we have claimed that the lyric form is today obsolete.

I have no doubt that the supreme love poets of our century, in English, are Hardy, Yeats, and Robert Graves. Hardy wrote at his finest, tenderest, most poignant—the poems of 1912–1913—after his first wife's death, when he was 72 years old. Is there a parallel in any literature to this winter-flower-

ing of a poetry of sentiment, which had lain dormant in the
poet's heart through the summer of his age, and was
awakened by the remorse Hardy felt over his long estrange-
ment from the woman who had died? If ever there was
"complete truth to feeling", it is in such poems as 'The
Going', 'After a Journey', 'At Castle Botcrel' and 'The
Voice':[3]

> Woman much missed, how you call to me, call to me,
> Saying that now you are not as you were
> When you had changed from the one who was all to me,
> But as at first, when our day was fair.
>
> Can it be you that I hear? Let me view you, then,
> Standing as when I drew near to the town
> Where you would wait for me: yea, as I knew you then,
> Even to the original air-blue gown . . .

Only four words of more than one syllable in these first two
stanzas: the poignant stress on the second 'then': the
dancing anapaestic rhythm slowed by the monosyllabic utterance and making a bitter-sweet marriage with the tone of
regret: the wraith-like, subjective mood suddenly pinned
down by one coloured, precise object—"the original air-
blue gown". Thus far, the poem is a pure lyric, and would be
complete in itself. But Hardy adds two stanzas, the first of
which questions the experience in a mildly rationalist way,
while in the second we have a change of metre and an image
of the poet "faltering forward" alone. Because of this, it is
a mixed poem, lyrical rather than lyric.

Yeats suffered a long apprenticeship to love in the person
of Maude Gonne: unrequited passion produced some fine
love poems of his middle period. But it was in old age that
he worked through to the lyric purity and starkness—love
poems which, like his late political ones, have the ballad
movement and, in contrast with Hardy's intimate recollec-

tions, are highly impersonal. The Crazy Jane poems, 'A
Last Confession', the Lady's three songs—these and many
others show the remarkable range of tone which Yeats
achieved in the lyric: the spiritual and the sexual, the eloquent and the ribald, are blended with extraordinary daring
—with the panache of a young man and the wisdom of an
old. But, to illustrate Yeats' mastery of the singing line, I
will take a less well-known lyric—a run-of-the-mill poem by
Yeats' standards—called 'Politics'.[4]

> How can I, that girl standing there,
> My attention fix
> On Roman or on Russian
> Or on Spanish politics?
> Yet here's a travelled man that knows
> What he talks about,
> And there's a politician
> That has read and thought,
> And maybe what they say is true
> Of war and war's alarms,
> But O that I were young again
> And held her in my arms!

The first thing to be noticed there is how Yeats can adapt
an easy, urbane conversational style to the demands of lyric.
It is achieved through his superb sense of rhythm, which
employs the small frequent changes of pace we would make,
saying the words in conversation, to produce a musical
ambience: we find ourselves, as we read the poem, all but
hearing a tune in the head. This is the true ballad touch;
and Yeats, having no ear for music, must have learnt it
from folk-ballads in the same way as we recognize it in such
poems of his—by attentive submission to the run of *words*.
If we were not tuned to the ballad style, we might make the
mistake of faulting this lyric for lack of intensity: one can
even imagine a dull critic cavilling at the slackness of "On

Roman or on Russian / Or on Spanish politics", and at the
superfluity in "Of war and war's alarms" ('alarms' just there
to make a rhyme). Such a critic—and I can assure you I
have seen similar obtusenesses in print—would merely prove
himself deaf to the hint of ballad refrain in those lines, and
to the ballad's general ranginess and open-work texture.

Second, the poem is lively yet flat —without rhetoric, without emotion, till the last two lines. It is not, and does not
pretend to be, a 'great poem': its specific gravity is unaltered
throughout. This all-of-a-pieceness we have seen again and
again as a quality of lyric. The tone here is one of insouci-
ance—of a gently mischievous irresponsibility (Yeats pre-
faced the poem by a reverberant quotation from Thomas
Mann: "In our time the destiny of man presents its meaning
in political terms"). And here is the great old poet, standing
in the political Thirties, with an eye for a girl and only
half an ear for the wiseacres—"But O that I were young
again / And held her in my arms": he is not solemn about
it, does not overvalue what is a real but momentary impulse,
and so the poem gives us complete truth to feeling.

Hardy and Yeats—they upset the common idea that lyrical
verse is a young man's medium. Robert Graves, again, has
written most of his love lyrics, and all the best of them, in
late middle age. The sequence of twenty-two love poems
printed in his More Poems 1961 combines austerity of
language with passionate violence of content, as Yeats does
in some of his Last Poems. Graves' is a classical spareness:
when I read 'The Intrusion', for instance, or 'Symptoms of
Love', the poet I am reminded of is Sappho— "Take courage,
lover! / Can you endure such grief / At any hand but hers."[5]
Yet these '1961' poems, for all their affinity with Greek minor
poetry, are truly modern and no one but Graves could have
written them. As an example of his lyric writing, however,
I would like to take a somewhat earlier poem, 'Counting the

Beats', which incidentally was chosen to be set to music by three composers for the Poetry Festival of 1963 in London.

You, love, and I,
(He whispers) you and I,
And if no more than only you and I
What can you or I?

Counting the beats,
Counting the slow heart beats,
The bleeding to death of time in slow heart beats,
Wakeful they lie.

Cloudless day,
Night, and a cloudless day;
Yet the huge storm will burst upon their heads one day,
From a bitter sky.

Where shall we be,
(She whispers) where shall we be,
When death strikes home, O where then shall we be
Who were you and I?

Not there but here,
(He whispers) only here,
As we are, here, together, now and here,
Always you and I.

Counting the beats,
Counting the slow heart beats,
The bleeding to death of time in slow heart beats,
Wakeful they lie.[6]

Love and death—the two deepest, most inexhaustible themes of poetry. Imagine earlier poets composing a poem on this heart-beat subject. A seventeenth century lyricist would, more likely than not, have made a Gather-ye-rosebuds variation of it; a Victorian would have played it for melancholy sentiment: neither, I fancy, could come as close to the marrow of the experience as does Robert Graves. I am not entirely happy about his first stanza—"And if no more than only you and I / What care you or I?" is a bit too near the merely ingenious verbal quibble. But after this, though there is constant repetition, there is no more quibbling; the cumulative refrains take over ("Counting the beats, / Counting the slow heart beats, / The bleeding to death of time in slow heart beats" . . .), remorselessly pointing the passage of life, the lovers' mortality. The poet is not afraid to use the absurd, brave clichés of a man comforting his beloved—"As we are, here together, now and here, / Always you and I." The movement of the verse is unvaryingly slow—slow, insistent, monotonous, like the ticking of a grandfather clock to one who lies in the dark, wakeful. Sparing of metaphor and epithet, an echo-chamber of refrain, the balance of lines and symmetry of stanzas satisfying the ear but never distracting the mind to admire technique when it should be absorbing experience, 'Counting the Beats' merges into one the systole and diastole of the heart, and the elemental response of lovers to their togetherness and their inevitable sundering.

A lyric is impersonal, not because the poet has deliberately screened personal feelings or memories out of it, but because he has broken *through them* to the ground of their being, a ground which is the fruitful compost made by numberless human experiences of a like nature. When we read these poems by Hardy, Yeats and Graves, we are quite willing to believe they underwent the particular experiences of love from which the poems arise: but their doing so is of no importance—it adds nothing either to the poem's value as poetry or its truth as a human testament. The breakthrough is a matter of skill, patience and luck—luck, grace, *curiosa felicitas,* whatever we call it, which is symbolised in the legend by the golden bridle. Just as scientists need to find the best way of talking about a problem in order to discover exactly what the problem is and thus work towards its solution, so the poet must develop a language that will enable him to make the break-through in his own sphere. A poet's language may become a highly personal one, like Yeats' or Hardy's; or it may be a common language, like that of the Caroline lyricists: but sooner or later a poetic language, like a scientific one, has to be changed, for the old one, whether individual or common, no longer serves to explore a problem and make a break-through.

Consider a poet born only eighteen years after Robert Graves—George Barker. He is the Dionysian type, rhapsodic, exuberant, hit-or-miss, but a serious and committed artist. His language has little in common with that of any predecessor: in 'Summer Song I' it produces a lyric which, unlike those of Hardy, Yeats, or Graves, has no visible thread of prose meaning running through it.

> *I looked into my heart to write*
> *And found a desert there.*
> *But when I looked again I heard*
> *Howling and proud in every word*
> *The hyena despair.*
>
> *Great summer sun, great summer sun,*
> *All loss burns in trophies;*
> *And in the cold sheet of the sky*
> *Lifelong the fishlipped lovers lie*
> *Kissing catastrophes.*
>
> *O loving garden where I lay*
> *When under the breasted tree*
> *My son stood up behind my eyes*
> *And groaned: Remember that the price*
> *Is vinegar for me.*

Great summer sun, great summer sun,
  Turn back to the designer:
I would not be the one to start
The breaking day and the breaking heart
  For all the grief in China.

My one, my one, my only love,
  Hide, hide your face in a leaf,
And let the hot tear falling burn
The stupid heart that will not learn
  The everywhere of grief.

Great summer sun, great summer sun,
  Turn back to the never-never
Cloud-cuckoo, happy far off land
Where all the love is true love, and
  True love goes on for ever.[7]

The language of this poem is certainly lyrical, so is its
rhythm, which keeps us moving ahead: although there are
some arresting phrases, we do not get those alternating
depths and shallows of meaning that vary the tempo at which
a poem runs through our mind. But towards what is it
moving? 'Summer Song' does not, as so many lyrics do,
anticipate at the start its inevitable resolution; nor, at the
end, are we quite sure what it all adds up to, for it is more
complex than the traditional lyric—complex by reason of
the erratic course of its images, and because it presents the
paradox of a desperate situation veiled in a confident almost
playful kind of language. It may be simply that Barker has
tried to say too many things in one poem. The poet's heart
is arid, with no voice except that of 'the hyena despair'
(stanza 1). Love is doomed to disaster, but in their sexual
trance lovers ('*kissing* catastrophes') refuse to admit it,
dazzled by the 'trophies' of love's war and not realising that
in the consummation of sexual love, love burns out and is
lost (stanza 2). The price of sexuality is paid by its fruit,

'my son', and is a bitter price (stanza 3). The poet tells the sun to 'turn back to the designer', God, and blames Him for 'the breaking day and the breaking heart' which the sunrise brings: this stanza simply won't do; the sun cannot turn back to the designer, except in the grossest pathetic fallacy; 'For all the grief in China' is meaningless and seems to be there only for the rhyme's sake. Stanzas 5 and 6, on the other hand, are admirable: the beloved's tears must teach him that grief is everywhere; he would like to return to the lover's fantasy world "where all the love is true love, and / True love goes on for ever". It's a lot of different things to say in thirty lines.

Barker's theme here is essentially the same as Graves' in 'Counting the Beats'—the transience of human love. But he over-elaborates it, and digresses too often from the central meaning: we are aware of a strong centrifugal force in the poem, pulling it in different directions. His method of controlling this force and keeping the poem's integrity relies too much on merely verbal associations—'all loss *burns* in trophies', 'let the hot tear falling *burn*'; 'the breasted *tree*', 'hide your face in a *leaf*', and so on. Hypnotic as the poem is, excellent though some of its stanzas are, "Summer Song' does not convince me, as 'Counting the Beats' does, of complete truth to feeling. It certainly illustrates the difficulty a poet has today in subduing his sophistication to the simple needs of lyric; and it suggests that the rhapsodic—I mean the fragmentary, the confused, the disconnected, the exaggeratedly enthusiastic—may be the most dangerous relation of the lyric.

Turning to Apollonian verse, the general tendency of 'The Movement' of the Fifties—verse in which the ego is clamped severely down upon the id—is a relief after the excesses of the Dionysian. I admire the frequent technical brilliance, the lucid intelligence, the good sense and honesty that have gone to its making. It is, at least, *interesting* verse, though I do not find many poems from which I get more at a second or third reading than I got at the first; the goods are all in the shop window: and one may sigh for a little more of Byron's "expression of excited passion". Love is treated analytically or ironically for the most part, rather than lyrically. A wry and circumspect approach is unlikely to produce a love lyric. It is worth remarking, though I do not propose to advance any theories about it, how often the heroes of young novelists of the Fifties are deeply suspicious of love and reluctant to commit themselves to it—particularly to marriage: so, with their poet contemporaries, there's little of the lover's lyric unreason, his commitment, his throwing the hat over the windmill. Highly though they esteem W. B. Yeats, they do not repeat after him his prayer "That I may seem, though I die old, / A foolish, passionate man."[8]

Nevertheless, there are exceptions. D. J. Enright's 'Waiting for the Bus' is nearly a lyric and truly a poem of love, though addressed to an elderly woman glimpsed for a moment gazing into a shop window.

She hung away her years, her eyes grew young,
*   And filled the dress that filled the shop;*
Her figure softened into summer, though wind stung
*   And rain would never stop.*

*   A dreaming not worn out with knowing,*
A moment's absence from the watch, the weather.
*   I threw the paper down, that carried no such story,*
But roared for what it could not have, perpetual health and
*   liberty and glory.*
*   It whirled away, a lost bedraggled feather.*

Then have we missed the bus? Or are we sure which way the
*   wind is blowing?*[9]

That last line, with its facile colloquialism and perfunctory meaning, does nothing but harm to the poem. The first stanza, however, is very fine—beautifully balanced, sustaining the metaphor for three lines with great delicacy— a metaphor true to the poet's subject and his feeling about her, never obtrusive or contrived: "Her figure softened into summer" is exquisite. The second stanza has a proper touch of violence—Enright's indignation at the grandiose, futile claims of the newspaper compared with the woman's simple "dreaming not worn out with knowing" of herself as young in a new dress.

Enright's poem is not pure lyric, for the second stanza has a note of self-consciousness, interpreting the situation from outside rather than giving it from within. None of the five poems I have read, except perhaps for George Barker's, is impersonal in this sense—without a hint of interpretation —though the Yeats and Graves ones come very near it. And each of them is distinguished by a personal idiom within the lyric mode. If I had to choose a poem of our time which is simple, transparent, and impersonal after the purest lyric model, I would go to a popular song.

> *Where have all the flowers gone?*
> *Long time passing*
> *Where have all the flowers gone?*
> *Long time ago*
> *Where have all the flowers gone?*
> *Young girls picked them, every one.*
> *When will they ever learn,*
> *O when will they ever learn?*
>
> *Where have all the young girls gone?*
> *Long time passing*
> *Where have all the young girls gone?*
> *Long time ago.*
> *Where have all the young girls gone?*
> *Gone to young men, every one.*
> *When will they ever learn,*
> *O when will they ever learn?*

Where have all the young men gone?
Gone for soldiers, every one . . .

Where have all the soldiers gone?
Gone to graveyards, every one . . .

Where have all the graveyards gone?
Gone to flower every one . . .

Where have all the flowers gone?*

You see?—it can be done even today: a poem with the simplicity of a nursery rhyme, the emotional charge of lyric. There's no logic about it; the refrains, "Long time passing" and "Long time ago", don't answer the questions; but they do respond to them, and with an emotional rightness. The words are greatly enhanced by the haunting tune—in its unpretentious way, it is a perfect marriage—yet, separated from the music, they have a life of their own. And I do not get the impression that 'Where have all the flowers gone' is an anachronism, a pastiche of folk-song.

When Mr. Seeger wrote and composed this song, the goddess surely lent him her golden bridle. Indeed, I am inclined to think that in the contemporary American folk-song, with its simplicity, vigour and inventiveness, lies the greatest hope for the lyric tradition.

Mr. Donald Davie has said somewhere that the modern poet "must grow ever more self-conscious, ever more aware of his bewilderingly diverse cultural heritage". This may be true in general; but I hope it should not be applied over the whole range of poetry, for, if it were, it would put the lyric out of business. I doubt whether being aware of his bewilderingly diverse cultural heritage will enable a poet to write better lyric; I am sure that, in the act of writing one, he must

---

* "Where Have All the Flowers Gone?" by Peter Seeger. © Copyright 1961 by Fall River Music Inc. All rights reserved. Used by permission.

leave his cultural heritage to look after itself: an awareness of Petrarch as the father of European lyric, of the relevance of the songs in Shakespeare's plays, of the contributions made by Po Chü-i or Pasternak, of Blake's symbolism, Ronsard's rhythms, Catullus' innovations, Seferis' personal mythology—such awareness is peripheral to the nature and needs of lyric. I distrust these large critical prescriptions for the health of poetry. A poet writing lyric, so it seems to me, must disinvolve himself from the intellectual subtleties and complex verbal plays which other kinds of verse may properly exploit today. He has to communicate with poetry's primal source *directly*, not through the diverse traditions into which that source has been channelled: I do not mean that his verse should be bardic, or surrealist, but that he recognise and submit to the lyric impulse, when it comes his way— the impulse to grieve or to rejoice singlemindedly, to discover images and rhythms which convey the elemental states of mind a man shares with all other living men and has in common with his remotest ancestors.

He must avoid the temptation to be 'modern' for the sake of being modern, and the vice of craving for 'originality'. Yet he cannot be content with pastiche of any lyric style of the past: he has to find new bottles for a wine which is timeless, new forms and new turns of language to replace those in which the Caroline lyricists, for example, conveyed their gaiety or Blake his profound intimations. He must have an instinct, an ear and a love for the singing line so that, although the old partnership with music is broken, in speaking a poem of his we are haunted by the ghost of a tune, a dancing rhythm, the felt presence of that universal melody— however faint it be today—through which primitive man expressed communion with his fellows and the joy of living.

To return for a little to the golden bridle, relating it with my own experience in the making of a poem. The bridle, as something which both releases and restrains, was *given* to Bellerophon. For me, many—but certainly not all—poems begin with a *donnée*, a phrase or line which comes to me out of the blue, and often bears no apparent relation with the field of experience I am involved in or meditating at the time. Here are a few examples. During the last war, this line came unbidden into my head—"The flags, the roundabouts, the gala day." It seemed like a riddle, an oracle. What sort of poem was it pointing to? Contemplating this enigmatic line, I became aware that it was charged with a kind of childish expectation and excitement; and out of this seed grew a sonnet about childhood— a subject I had rarely attempted before: it was as though the violent happenings of war, together with a private emotional crisis of my own, had like an earthquake thrown up strata of my early experience which, till then, had not been available to me as a poet. And out of that sonnet grew a sequence of nine sonnets expressing, through images only, states of mind connected with childhood, adolescence, and middle age.

Or again, I was sitting inoffensively in my study one day, when I received—out of the blue—three words, "To taste myself." A very curt and curious evangel. Well, I worked down into it: and the result was a poem, 'The Room', which beneath the fable of a prince who must retire now and then from public affairs into a secret room of the palace (. . . "he went there / Simply to taste himself, to be reassured / That under the royal action and abstraction / He lived in, he was real."[10])—under this guise, expressed my own need for solitude, to withdraw from the demands and irrelevancies to which even a poet is subjected when he becomes, in however small a way, a public figure.

Those two *données* had nothing to do with what I was thinking about at the time they came. There is also the *donnée* which, though still a riddle, *is* connected with a present preoccupation. A few years ago I was thinking about

possessiveness— how, in my younger days, I had travelled
light and despised the way my elders seemed to cherish, even
to identify themselves with, their material possessions. And
suddenly there swam into my head the phrase "Streamlined
whales and hulls." Very pretty, but what on earth had it to
do with the subject of my vague contemplation? Still, I'd
better follow it up and see what happened. What happened
was

> *Think of streamlined whales and hulls*
> *Accumulating barnacles*
> *By moving long enough immersed*
> *In their own element.*

Ah, there it was—the clogging effect of barnacles, of possessions! And the lines have their place now in the middle of a
long poem, a marine allegory called "Travelling Light."[11]

One more example. For some time I had wanted to write
an elegy for a certain woman I had never met personally, but
had heard about from her widower—a brave and fascinating
woman who had died of a hideous disease. But I could not
find a way into the subject. Then on the island of Delos,
communing with those beautiful, weather-beaten stone lions
(who, if I may say so, are now old friends of mine), I
heard—almost as if the lions had spoken it out of the island's
holy hush, "Not the silence after music, but the silence of
no more music." To me, those words had an extraordinary
momentousness. I connected them at once with the dead
woman; and the elegy began to get written.

A *donnée*, then, suggests a way into the unwritten poem.
But it may also come after a poem has been started—when
I have tried several avenues of approach maybe, and left them
open: I am still undecided as to what the growing poem is
really about, what is the theme which should underlie and
emerge through the tangled mass of subject matter. Here,
the *donnée* points decisively the way the poem should go;

and often this will mean taking the poem to bits and starting again. I need hardly say that these enticing *données* will sometimes prove to be will-o-the-wisps and land one deeper into the bog; they must be judged in the light of the growing poem as a whole.

So much for the golden bridle as a charm which releases a poem into movement. What about its restraining function? I myself see the bridle, from this aspect, as a symbol of poetic form. Paul Valéry wrote somewhere: "Why do I use strict form? To prevent the poem saying everything". That is an extremely profound remark. A poetic form (which conveniently rhymes with 'norm') provides the poet with a system of checks and balances external to the memories, thoughts, images, which an incipient poem catches, and which—if not controlled—may run away with it. The form is a discipline which helps to select from an incoherent mass of material those data that are relevant to the poem's still undecided purpose. But the form is not always merely selective and disciplinary: many poets must have observed in their own work, as Valéry did, that the need for a rhyme in a certain place, or the exigency of a metre, has thrown up a revealing phrase, a creative idea, which might well not have come into existence without the prompting of the formal agency. Form, in a word, not only restrains but stimulates.

When my youngest son was born, seven years ago, filled with euphoria I dashed off on a poem about this event, a poem in four-line rhyming stanzas. I had not gone far when the poem stalled. I raised the hood and examined the engine: it had seized up—yes, obviously; but what should I do next? I decided to start again, with—so to speak—a new engine. Perhaps I could distance myself from my still raw emotions by employing a more complex stanza form. So, for the four-line stanza I substituted one of ten lines, rhyming *a b b a c d b c d b*. There were still several misadventures on the way; but the poem, 'The Newborn', got to its destination. The recalcitrance of this more elaborate form enabled me to distance my emotions and go deeper into the heart of the experience from which they had sprung: by deliberately placing technical difficulties in my way, I had made it easier to find and pursue the right path.

Every poem has the potentiality to be a unique creation, though few of them realise their potentiality. One sets a form: the poem, growing inside it, learning its own specific nature and gradually seeing clearer its destination, will cause one to modify in the light of this increasing self-knowledge the form one has roughed out for it. Don't think of poetic form as a bed of Procrustes, cutting down the subject or racking it out to some pre-fixed dimensions. Think of it as the golden bridle which, in concentrating energy, stimulates and releases energy.

I would like to sum all this up in one stanza of a poem written shortly after I arrived in Cambridge last October.

> *Unwritten poems loom as if*
> *They'd cover the whole of earthly life.*
> *But each one, growing, learns to trim its*
> *Impulse and meaning to the limits*
> *Roughed out by me, then modified*
> *In its own truth's expanding light.*
> *A poem, settling to its form,*
> *Finds there no jailer, but a norm*
> *Of conduct, and a fitting sphere*
> *Which stops it wandering everywhere.*

The Muse, though she visit her poet but fitfully, is the ground of his being. She will not come meekly to his call; but when she does come, she possesses him entire, and her absence leaves a void which cannot be filled with other preoccupations. He may have no religious belief, may even feel no need for a god, yet he is religious in the sense that he cannot live by material values: though he may not know it, he is the man in Browning's poem—the one "Through a whole campaign of the world's life and death,/Doing the King's work all the dim day long".

To him, that work is one of interpretation and creation, and the two are inseparable. He has to make out of words an object which is distanced from his own personal experience, yet by indirections will make sense of it and communicate the feeling of it. A poem's meaning is what happens when the feeling and the sense are fused: it does not explain, it satisfies. The child, playing with stones, makes a pattern. To write a poem is an act of serious play.

Because they seldom seem to get to the heart of this paradox (after all, it is their job to study the pattern, not the pattern-maker), our poet finds literary critics rather unhelpful. They tell him what is wrong with a poem he has written, or what would have been right with the poem he should have written: but he is not concerned with that poem any more; he wants advice about the one he is writing now. So he must fall back upon self-criticism, at which he is not always very expert. At best, it is a hand-to-mouth affair—a matter of watching attentively for those signs which tell him a poem should change course, or return to port and start again, or of carrying out running repairs on a vessel which is in motion.

Again, he finds much of this talk about 'the intentional fallacy' either wrong headed or beside the point. When he begins a lyric poem, his intention is not at all clear to him: if he is skillful and lucky, the poem will begin to reveal to him his intention, and its theme, as he works upon it. The finished poem is a harmony (or discord) between his own meaning and the meanings his readers receive from it. *His* is a meaning, admittedly, clarified out of an intention which is vague; but it is not to be dismissed therefore as irrelevant, either in considering the poem as a whole or a given part of it. A critic (who, being himself a poet, should have known better) recently declared that Hopkins' phrase, 'Shook foil', refers to fencing. On its being pointed out that Hopkins, in a letter to Bridges, said he was thinking of tin-foil paper, this critic unabashedly reaffirmed his own interpretation, saying that to accept Hopkins' statement was to succumb to the intentional fallacy. It is not so much the fact that the critic's interpretation goes dead against the grain of the poem, but the critical conceit of ruling a poet's own evidence out of court, which one finds so deplorable.

A man sings in the bath, partly because its walls flatter his voice, giving it unusual resonance, but chiefly because warm water (who ever sings in a cold bath?) reminds him of his origin, relaxes inhibitions, recalls a primary, instinctual self. It is this self, I believe, from which the lyric impulse arises and the singing line proceeds. Of course, our poet is no singer-in-a-bath; but, however he may sophisticate his utterance, it will be a lyrical one provided he has made contact with what, in nature and human nature, is spontaneous. Whether he celebrates love or grief, living or dying, at the source of his poem and permeating it throughout is the element of joy—the joy of responding to life by making patterns from a chaos.

In any lyric poem we feel perhaps a touch of irresponsibility. Life isn't so simple as all that, we may protest: what about the Bomb? malnutrition? the dangers of smoking? the divorce figures? Freud, and the marvels of technology, and the expanding universe? And here's this child, playing with coloured pebbles, expecting us to take him seriously! A touch of irresponsibility? our poet replies: what you are feeling is the touch of joy; and my play is serious. I am playing to delight and console you—myself and you. My pebbles can be a causeway, reuniting your divided self, and my own. Every good work of every artist is there to remind man of his roots, to refresh them, to satisfy—if only for a few years or hours— his perpetual need for wholeness.

NOTES   INDEX

NOTES

CHAPTER 1: THE LYRIC IMPULSE

1. Robert Finch, *Poems* (Toronto: Oxford University Press, 1946).
2. Campion and Rosseter's *Book of Airs*.
3. From *Collected Poems of William Butler Yeats* (1933, 1956). Reprinted with permission of Macmillan Co. Ltd. of London, The Macmillan Co. of New York, and Mrs. Bertha Georgie Yeats.

CHAPTER 2: WORDS AND MUSIC

1. Peter Pears, The Aldeburgh Festival Programme Book, 1963.
2. John Stevens, *Music and Poetry in the Early Tudor Court* (London, 1961; University of Nebraska Press, 1963).
3. Bruce Pattison, *Music and Poetry of the English Renaissance* (London: Methuen, 1948).
4. *Ibid.*
5. *Ibid.*
6. V. C. Clinton-Baddeley, *Words for Music* (Cambridge University Press, 1941).
7. Pattison, *Music and Poetry of the English Renaissance*.
8. W. B. Yeats, Preface to *A Broadside*, ed. W. B. Yeats and Dorothy Wellesley (Dublin: Cuala Press, 1937)
9. From "Into my heart an air that kills", from "A Shropshire Lad", *Collected Poems* of A. E. Housman (London: Jonathan Cape, 1939; New York: Holt, Rinehart and Winston, Inc., 1940). Quoted by permission of the Society of Authors, London, as representatives of the Estate of the late A. E. Housman, and by permission of Holt, Rinehart and Winston, Inc.
10. Clinton-Baddeley, *Words for Music*.
11. Pattison, *Music and Poetry of the English Renaissance*.
12. From *Collected Poems* by William Butler Yeats (1933, 1956). Reprinted with permission of Macmillan Co. Ltd. of London, The Macmillan Co. of New York, and Mrs. Bertha Georgie Yeats.

13. From *Collected Poems* of C. Day Lewis, 2nd ed. (London: Jonathan Cape and Hogarth Press, 1954.

14. *Ibid.*

CHAPTER 3: THE STORY LYRIC

1. M. J. C. Hodgart, *The Ballad* (London: Hutchinson, 1950).

2. Karen Blixen, *Out of Africa* (London: Putnam & Co. Ltd., 1937; New York: Random House, 1938).

3. G. H. Gerould, *The Ballad of Tradition* (Oxford: Clarendon Press, 1932; New York: Oxford University Press, 1957).

4. Willa Muir, *Living with Ballads* (London: Hogarth Press, and New York: Oxford University Press, 1965).

5. Iona and Peter Opie, *The Lore and Language of Schoolchildren* (1959). Quoted by permission of the Clarendon Press, Oxford.

6. Blixen, *Out of Africa.*

7. Edwin Muir, *The Estate of Poetry* (London: Faber and Faber; Cambridge, Mass.: Harvard University Press, 1962).

8. Gerould, *The Ballad of Tradition.*

9. *Ibid.* Lines from "Child Waters" are reprinted by permission of the Clarendon Press, Oxford, England, and Oxford University Press, New York.

10. L. C. Wimberly, *Folklore in the English and Scottish Ballads* (Chicago, 1928).

11. Gerould, *The Ballad of Tradition.*

12. "The Foreboding", from *Collected Poems* of Robert Graves (London: Cassell, 1948; New York: Doubleday, 1955). © International Authors N. V. 1956, 1959, and 1961. Quoted by permission of International Authors N. V., owners of Mr. Graves' copyright.

13. From *Collected Shorter Poems* of W. H. Auden (New York: Random House, 1945; London: Faber and Faber, 1949).

14. From *Collected Poems* of Louis MacNeice (London: Faber and Faber, 1949; New York: Oxford University Press, 1963).

15. Charles Causley, *Johnny Alleluia* (London: Rupert Hart-Davis, 1961).

CHAPTER 4: THE COMMON MUSE

1. V. de S. Pinto and A. E. Rodway, *The Common Muse* (London: Chatto and Windus, 1957; New York: Philosophical Library).

2. W. Henderson, *Victorian Street Ballads* (London: Country Life, 1937).

3. From C. O'Lochlainn, *Irish Street Ballads* (Dublin: Sign of the Three Candles; London: Constable, 1939; New York: Corinth Books, 1960).

4. A. L. Lloyd, *Come All Ye Bold Miners* (London: Lawrence & Wishart, 1952).

5. Pinto and Rodway, *The Common Muse*.
6. From *Collected Poems* of Louis MacNeice (London: Faber and Faber, 1949; New York: Oxford University Press, 1963).
7. O'Lochlainn, *Irish Street Ballads*.
8. *Ibid.*
9. C. Day Lewis, *A Hope for Poetry* (Oxford, Basil Blackwell, 1934; New York: Random House, 1935).
10. From *Collected Poems* of Louis MacNeice.
11. From *Collected Shorter Poems* of W. H. Auden (New York: Random House, 1945; London: Faber and Faber, 1950).
12. L. C. A. Knowles, *The Industrial and Commercial Revolutions in Great Britain during the Nineteenth Century* (London: Routledge & Kegan Paul, 1921).
13. From *The Complete Poems* of D. H. Lawrence, 3 vols. (London: Heinemann, 1957; New York, Viking, 1964). By permission of Laurence Pollinger Ltd. and the Estate of the late Mrs. Frieda Lawrence.
14. From *Collected Poems* of Edwin Muir (London: Faber and Faber, 1960).

CHAPTER 5: COUNTRY LYRICS

1. Joseph Warren Beach, *The Concepts of Nature in Nineteenth-Century English Poetry* (New York, 1936).
2. Thomas Blackburn, *The Price of an Eye* (London: Longmans, Green, 1961; New York, William Morrow). © Copyright 1961 by William Morrow & Co. Inc., New York, N. Y.
3. "The New Nature Poetry", The American Scholar, 1959.
4. From "The Wood Pile", from *The Complete Poems of Robert Frost* (London: Jonathan Cape; New York: Holt, Rinehart and Winston, 1960). Reprinted with permission of the publishers.
5. Charles Davy, *Words in the Mind* (London: Chatto and Windus, 1965).
6. *Ibid.*
7 "A Grave", from *Collected Poems* by Marianne Moore (London: Faber and Faber; New York: The Macmillan Co., 1951). Reprinted with permission of the publishers.
8. From "The Need of Being Versed in Country Things", from *The Complete Poems of Robert Frost* (London: Jonathan Cape; New York: Holt, Rinehart and Winston, Inc, 1960). Reprinted with permission of the publishers.
9. *The Poems of John Clare*, ed. J. W. Tibble (London: J. M. Dent, 1935.
10. *Ibid.*

11. From *The Collected Poems* of Thomas Hardy (London, 1919; New York, 1961). Reprinted with permission of the Trustees of the Hardy Estate, Macmillan Co. Ltd. of London, The Macmillan Co. of Canada, Ltd., and The Macmillan Co., New York.

12. J. W. Tibble, Introduction to *The Poems of John Clare*.

13. *Ibid.*

14. Thomas Hardy (ed.) in his Preface to *Select Poems of William Barnes* (n.d.) Quoted by permission of the Clarendon Press, Oxford.

CHAPTER 6: THE GOLDEN BRIDLE

1. Roy Campbell, *Adamastor* (London: Faber and Faber, 1930). Reprinted with permission of Curtis, Brown Ltd., London.

2. John Press, *Rule and Energy* (London: Oxford University Press, 1963).

3. "The Voice", from *Collected Poems* by Thomas Hardy (London, 1919; New York, 1961. Reprinted with permission of the Trustees of the Hardy Estate, Macmillan Co. Ltd. of London, The Macmillan Co. of Canada, Ltd., and The Macmillan Co. of New York.

4. "Politics", from *Collected Poems* by William Butler Yeats (1933, 1956). Reprinted with permission of Macmillan Co. Ltd. of London, The Macmillan Co. of New York, and Mrs. Bertha Georgie Yeats.

5. "Symptoms of Love", from *More Poems 1961* by Robert Graves (London: Cassell; New York: Doubleday & Co.). © International Authors N. V., 1956, 1959, and 1961. By permission of International Authors, N. V., owners of Mr. Graves' copyright.

6. "Counting the Beats", from *Collected Poems* of Robert Graves (London: Cassell, 1948; New York: Doubleday, 1955). © International Authors N. V., 1956, 1959, and 1961. By permission (see previous note).

7. "Summer Song", from *Collected Poems* of George Barker (London: Faber and Faber, 1957; New York: Clarke and Way, 1958).

8. From *Collected Poems* by William Butler Yeats (see n. 4 above).

9. "Waiting for the Bus", from *The Laughing Hyena* by D. J. Enright (London: Routledge & Kegan Paul, 1953).

10. From *Requiem for the Living* by C. Day Lewis (New York: Harper & Row, 1964).

11. "Travelling Light", from *Requiem for the Living*; in England, from *The Gate* by C. Day Lewis (London: Jonathan Cape, 1962).

INDEX